— Missouri*Life* —

LEWIS AND CLARK'S JOURNEY ACROSS MISSOURI

— Missouri*Life* —

LEWIS AND CLARK'S
JOURNEY
ACROSS MISSOURI

A special commemorative publication of Missouri Life

Editor
Sona Pai

Art Director
Drew Barton

Primary Author and Photographer
Brett Dufur

Contributing Authors
Jo Beck, James Denny, J. Frederick Fausz,
Sadie Grabill, Claire Griffis, Kathy Love,
Erwin Neighbors, Ann Rogers, Lowell Schake

Contributing Photographers
Scott R. Avetta, Glenn Curcio, Sylvia Forbes,
Mike Heimos, Don Kurz, Elizabeth McDonald,
John Seals, Kevin Sink

Original maps
James Harlan

Editorial Assistants
Martha Knight and Sadie Grabill

— Missouri*Life* magazine—

President and Publisher
Greg Wood
greg@missourilife.com

Editor in Chief
Danita Allen Wood
danita@missourilife.com

Managing Editor
Martha Everett
martha@missourilife.com

Art Director
Drew Barton

Director of Advertising
Deborah Marshall
deborah@missourilife.com

Circulation Manager
Colleen Mahon
colleen@missourilife.com

Calendar and Advertising Coordinator
Amy Stapleton
amy@missourilife.com

Web Editor
Malcolm White

MissouriLife magazine celebrates the unique people and places of Missouri, past and present. For information, or to subscribe:

E-mail: info@missourilife.com

Phone: 800-492-2593, ext. 101 or 102

Fax: 660-248-2310

Web site: www.missourilife.com

Address: 112 E. Morrison Street, Fayette, MO 65248

Near St. Louis, Missouri, May 20, 1804

"At half after one P.M. our progress was interrupted the near approach of a violent thunder storm from the N.W. and concluded to take shelter in a little cabbin hard by untill the rain should be over. ... The clouds continued to follow each other in rapaid succession, insomuch that there was little prospect of it's ceasing to rain this evening; as I had determined to reach St. Charles this evening and knowing that there was now no time to be lost I set forward in the rain, most of the gentlemen continued with me, we arrived at half after six and joined Capt. Clark, found the party in good health and sperits. —Meriwether Lewis

REDISCOVER LEWIS AND CLARK'S MISSOURI

By **James Denny**

Historian, Missouri Department of Natural Resources, Division of State Parks

O N JANUARY 18, 1803, President Thomas Jefferson sent a confidential message to the U.S. Congress in which he proposed an extraordinary exploratory enterprise: "An intelligent officer with ten or twelve chosen men might explore the whole line [of the continent], even to the Western ocean. ..." Jefferson already had an intelligent officer in mind — his secretary, Capt. Meriwether Lewis. Within a few months, Lewis's friend, William Clark, would sign on as co-leader. Congress appropriated twenty-five hundred dollars for the venture, and Lewis immediately began to make extensive preparations for the journey.

On the day Lewis was getting ready to set off for Pittsburgh, July 4, 1803, he learned the astounding news of the Louisiana Purchase. On April 31, France had conveyed to the United States all of the lands that drained into the west side of the Mississippi River and all of the lands draining into the Missouri River. The tract contained more than 828,000 square miles and was purchased at the bargain price of fifteen million dollars. The fledgling nation doubled in size after this extraordinary land deal.

The expedition Jefferson was about to send up the Missouri River would now take on a whole new importance. Much of Jefferson's new land acquisition had never been seen by Western eyes. These lands and the plants and animals that dwelt there would need to be described for science, and maps and numerous measurements of latitude and longitude would need to be made to fix the boundaries of the new domain. There were powerful Indian nations living within the new territory, and economic and diplomatic ties would have to be established with them. The Missouri River, most of its length still shrouded in mystery, needed to be followed to its source. The route across the continent to the Pacific had to be explored to find out once and for all whether the fabled Northwest Passage actually existed.

The stage was set for America's greatest exploration adventure —

THE HISTORIC JOURNEY BEGAN AND ENDED IN THE SHOW-ME STATE

In Missouri, Lewis and Clark encountered water that was rough at times but smooth as glass at others. They also enjoyed lush landscapes, gentle breezes, and stunning sunsets on the river.

the Lewis and Clark expedition. The bicentennial of the journey is upon us, and the national commemoration is well underway. Public and private agencies have been planning for this event for years, and every state along the Lewis and Clark trail will hold special events from 2004 to 2006.

This renewed interest in Lewis and Clark is largely a twentieth century phenomenon. It was not until 1903, a full century after the expedition, that the complete journals of the Lewis and Clark expedition were finally published, and the public could, for the first time, have direct access to the extraordinary accounts of the "writingest explorers of all time." In the century that has followed, popular interest in Lewis and Clark has grown enormously. The Lewis and Clark expedition has exerted a powerful grip on the historical imagination of the nation. The saga of the adventure has become our American Odyssey, the quintessential telling of our national tale of westward yearning.

Scientists and Diplomats
At the turn of the nineteenth century, the American West was still one of the most mysterious and inaccessible regions on earth. Since

the 1500s, mapmakers had left the northwestern quadrant of the continent blank, or they filled in the area with fanciful geographical speculations that kept alive the longed-for promise of an easy passage to the Pacific Ocean. In April 1805, the Lewis and Clark expedition pulled out from its winter haven at the villages of the hospitable Mandan Indians, located sixteen hundred miles up the Missouri River, and they plunged into the unknown reaches of an immense tract of unexplored country. Leaving supply lines and communication with the outside world far behind, they traveled twenty-four hundred miles through lands that had never been seen by Western eyes. They would not be heard from for more than a year, and everyone but Jefferson gave them up for dead.

By the time of their triumphant return to St. Louis, September 23, 1806, Lewis and Clark had succeeded in lifting that cloak of mystery that had so long hung like a mist over the lands that lay up the Missouri and beyond the numerous mountains. Clark produced his masterful and detailed map of the West, and Lewis's vivid journal descriptions brought to life the magnificence of the sights he saw: the endless prairies filled with vast herds of buffalo; the grotesque cliffs of the Missouri Breaks country and the breathtak-

Many of the crew members in the Corps of Discovery would decide to stay in Missouri after the expedition returned in 1806.

ing first sighting of the Great Falls of the Missouri River in present-day Montana; the forbidding, snow-capped ranges of the nearly impenetrable mountains of the Bitterroot Range; the mighty Columbia River; and the pounding surf of the Pacific Ocean.

The Lewis and Clark expedition was the nation's first military and scientific expedition, and as such it was an astounding success. Seldom has the world seen such a remarkable report of a scientific journey as in the million words contained in the explorers' collected journals. They include descriptions of 178 plants that were new to science and 122 previously unknown animals, such as prairie dogs, the Lewis woodpecker, and the grizzly bear.

Among the most important observations were of the nearly fifty Indian tribes the explorers encountered. Jefferson had given Lewis a detailed list of the type of information he and his science-minded friends wanted to know about American Indians, including population, language, economic activities, customs and dress, diseases, and religion.

Beyond science, Lewis and Clark had an important diplomatic and economic mission in their Indian relations. When the United States acquired the Louisiana Territory, the country also inherited the land inhabited by numerous and powerful Indian tribes. Lewis and Clark now had to inform these incredulous tribes that they had

just been traded to a new international power, the United States, and that they were now the "children" of a new great father, Thomas Jefferson. The chiefs could gaze on the president's benevolent profile, which was embossed on the peace medals they received from Lewis and Clark, along with an invitation to visit the great man in Washington, D.C., and behold the overwhelming population, might, and empire of their new protectors.

If these encounters were less than ideal from the points of view of either the tribes on the riverbank or the captains coming upriver to meet them, it is because neither group understood the other very well. Beyond that, the captains were dealing with Indians who were shrewd, seasoned traders. It would take more than beads and peace medals to win over these proud warriors. Like all of their tribal neighbors, they wanted guns so that they could gain preeminence in the new arms race that was brewing on the plains as a result of stiff competition between Western countries for Indian loyalty and trade.

Even so, a fact that is at the heart of the modern bicentennial observations is that the Lewis and Clark expedition would not have succeeded without the help of many Indian nations, especially the Mandans, Shoshone, and Nez Percé. It was not just Sacagawea single-handedly pointing the forward course that got the expedition through, but also Mandan corn and hospitality, and Shoshone and Nez Percé horses and guides. Because of the ambivalent long-term consequences of the expedition for Indians, the present observance is referred to as a commemoration rather than a celebration. The American Indian experience at the hands of Lewis and Clark's successors over the last two centuries is hardly something to celebrate.

Missouri's Part of the Story

At the starting and ending points of the expedition lay the lands that would become part of the state of Missouri, and yet sometimes, it seems like Missouri is short-changed in some tellings of the Lewis and Clark adventure. One condensation of the "complete" journals only devotes seventeen out of 382 pages to the portion of the journey that took place in present Missouri. That this has happened may be a byproduct of Lewis's failure to produce a published account of the expedition. By the time interest in the expedition was rekindled in the early twentieth century, the last frontiers had closed.

The era of continental expansion that began with Lewis and Clark from 1804 to 1806 was over by the 1890s, and in the rush of nostalgia about the end of the Wild West, the rich history at the eastern end of the Lewis and Clark trail became less important than encounters with exotic Indians, ferocious grizzly bears, endless herds of buffalo, and high, snowy mountains. By the time the details of the Missouri story became available in the first printed edition of the journals, after 1903, no one seemed very interested in connecting with that story.

As we come to better understand Missouri's key role in the expedition, the process can be a thrilling journey of rediscovery in its own right — our state has a great Lewis and Clark story to tell. It started on November 16, 1803, when Lewis and Clark left their camp at the junction of the Ohio and Mississippi Rivers, crossed to the "Spanish" side of the river, and took their first footsteps on the soil of the Louisiana Purchase. Along the Mississippi, they met Shawnee Indians living peacefully with the large numbers of newly arrived Americans who were already pouring into the region.

They spent December 1803 to May 1804 in winter camp, with the group of hardy woodsmen and crack army soldiers that had been selected by the captains to form the Corps of Discovery. During this period, one or both of the captains were in St. Louis purchasing a long list of supplies, including Indian gifts acquired from leading merchants such as Auguste and Pierre Chouteau. In this vibrant community, they talked with traders who had been far up the Missouri and could report the very latest information about the Missouri River and the Indian tribes they could expect to meet. They took time off, on March 9 and 10, 1804, to witness the ceremony that transferred the Louisiana Territory from Spain to France to the United States.

The captains hired a crew of experienced French river men who were recruited from St. Louis and St. Charles. Many of these men,

including their great hunter and interpreter George Drouillard, had French fathers and Indian mothers. The expedition that headed up the Missouri River on May 14, 1804, was international in its make-up and reflected the colorful mix of cultures that had gained a foothold along the margins of the Mississippi and Missouri Rivers.

Roaring River and Lush Land

The six hundred miles of the Missouri River within the modern border of the state presented the first challenge of the many the expedition would face. The Missouri was the most difficult to navigate of western rivers. Its current could race along at a fast seven or eight miles an hour and kick up rapids that "rored like an immence falls." Sandbars that could sink a boat would form and dissolve in the rushing currents to re-form somewhere else. Sections of the riverbank, trees and all, could suddenly heave into the churning waters of the rapidly flowing river. Spear-like snags and sawyers reared above the foaming current. It took everything the crews of the keelboat and two pirogues had to work the expedition flotilla up the mighty river.

On rare days they could sail under a favoring wind, but usually they were pulling at oars, leaning into poles, or if all else failed, straining on a tow rope to coax the boats upstream. "It can hardly be imagined the fataigue we underwent," lamented Pvt. Joseph Whitehouse after one in a succession of hot, exhausting days in which the men were pushed to the limits of endurance trying to move the boats foot by hard-fought foot up the unforgiving river.

The men quickly transformed themselves from inexperienced river men into seasoned veterans. So impressed was Clark by their performance that he boasted, "I can Say with Confidence that our party is not inferior to any that was ever on the waters of the Missoppie." With tough and devoted men such as these, Lewis and Clark knew they could face any challenge that lay before them.

As the expedition moved up the Mississippi and Missouri Rivers, the men were keenly attuned to the richness and fertility of the forested and prairie country they saw. That Missouri was a veritable Garden of Eden is a theme that is sounded by all of the journal keepers. This was perfect country for yeoman farmers, and in Jefferson's mind a land inhabited by farmers living on their own homesteads was a land where democracy would flourish for generations to come. Lewis and Clark, in their post-expedition careers as territorial governors, would help lay the foundations of this agricultural empire.

This bicentennial of those foundational events of our history — the Louisiana Purchase and the Lewis and Clark expedition — is a good time to take stock of the country that the Corps of Discovery explored and we inherited. Follow their trail along the great rivers and seek out your own adventure along the many scenic highways that etch their way through the big river country. You just may discover that Jefferson's dream is alive and well in Missouri.

AS WE COME TO BETTER UNDERSTAND MISSOURI'S KEY ROLE IN THE EXPEDITION, THE PROCESS CAN BE A THRILLING JOURNEY OF REDISCOVERY.

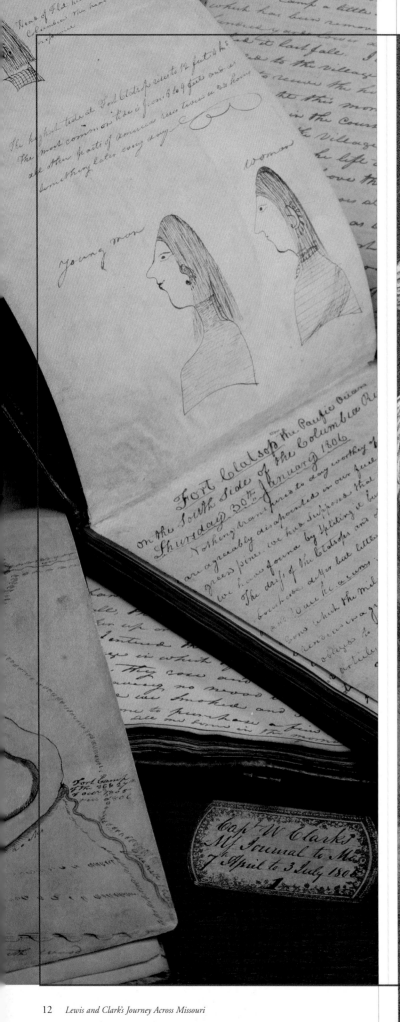

LE-SOL

AN

LEWIS AND CLARK IN MISSOURI

I N THE FIRST years of the nineteenth century, what we know today as Missouri was a mystery to most Americans. The lands that include our state had been passed back and forth between the Spanish and the French, and the American population was concentrated in the east, near the Atlantic Ocean. President Thomas Jefferson was acutely aware that the land that stretched beyond the Mississippi River — the western boundary of the United States at the time — was full of potential for a young country ready to grow. With the Louisiana Purchase in 1803, Jefferson acquired the land between the Mississippi River and the Rocky Mountains, and he sent an expedition led by Meriwether Lewis and William Clark to explore the new western frontier.

On the pages that follow, we explore the expedition from Missouri's perspective. You'll see how the Missouri River has changed since the Corps of Discovery traveled on its waters, and you'll learn how you can plan your own expedition. Our stories explain how the Missouri and Osage Indians and the fur trade contributed to Missouri's culture, and how settlements like La Charrette impressed the explorers with their hospitality. You'll also meet the men Lewis and Clark assembled for the journey, many of whom remained in Missouri after the voyage.

Missourians were the last Americans Lewis and Clark would see on their way to the West and also the first to welcome them home. Today, Lewis and Clark's spirit of discovery continues to inspire Missourians. >>>

THE MISSOURI RIVER THEN AND NOW

By Brett Dufur

UNTIL THE EARLY nineteenth century, much of the land we now know as Missouri was inaccessible to most travelers. The Missouri River flowed through the area like a brushstroke of good fortune for the indigenous people and wildlife living near it, and river and land were connected in the grand cycle of life. Then, it was known as the *Pekitanoui,* an American Indian word for "muddy water." The people living along the river were known as the Missouri, meaning "the people of the big canoes," and some French explorers also knew the river by this name. The river flooded the lands seasonally and created a biologically rich stew that supported a multitude of flora and fauna. Imagine a river valley and the surrounding prairie teeming with life, with black bear, deer, bison, and elk. It was a veritable Garden of Eden. For the explorers and generations of pioneers to follow, the river would become our country's original superhighway, transforming American transportation, commerce, and communication.

The river valley had been inhabited by American Indians for centuries and had been explored by the French Canadians. But for the young United States, Meriwether Lewis, William Clark, and their Corps of Discovery were entering *terra incognita* when they set out on the river in 1804. The map of the American West was like a page from a coloring book, with defined edges and lots of white space in the middle, waiting for the explorers to fill it in. On what is considered one of the most successful military expeditions in history, the

LEWIS AND CLARK WOULDN'T RECOGNIZE THE RIVER TODAY

Corps of Discovery traveled close to eight thousand miles in two years and four months. During that time, they filled in the map of the western frontier and paved the way for expansion in the newly acquired Louisiana Territory.

A Road to the Mythical West

President Thomas Jefferson, who sent the men westward, believed they might find blue-eyed, Welsh-speaking Indians, Peruvian llamas, woolly mammoths, or even giant ground sloths. Expedition member Sgt. Patrick Gass wrote that he expected to confront "warlike savages of gigantic stature." Some of Jefferson's scholarly books proposed possible encounters with a landmass of erupting volcanoes and even mountains of undissolved salt. Other readings led Jefferson to believe that Virginia's Blue Ridge Mountains might be the continent's highest.

In 1803, such myths defined the uncharted American West. The Lewis and Clark expedition would later dispel the most widely held myth — the existence of a Northwest Passage — a coveted series of rivers that Jefferson hoped would connect the Atlantic Ocean to the Pacific Ocean by way of the Missouri River. At the time, only four roads crossed west of the Appalachian Mountains, and by horse, it was impossible to get anything from the Mississippi River to the Atlantic seaboard in fewer than six weeks. Jefferson saw that the best way to develop trade and the country would be to follow the Ohio and Mississippi Rivers down to the Gulf of Mexico, and the Missouri River, he hoped, all the way to the Pacific Ocean.

Clark and his men set out on May 14, 1804, from their winter camp at the mouth of the Wood River, crossed the Mississippi, and began the voyage up the Missouri River. Two days later, their keelboat and two smaller boats called pirogues would arrive twenty miles upriver at St. Charles. Lewis joined them on May 20 after taking care of some last-minute affairs in St. Louis. On May 21, at the St. Charles riverfront, the men shook hands and began their journey west together as Lewis and Clark, leaders of the Corps of Discovery.

The Missouri River that lay ahead of them was a vast series of interconnected, braided streams, stretching more than a mile wide at places with a shallow, slow-moving wetland buffering the edges of its unpredictable and meandering main channel. It was a maze of sandbars, collapsing banks, and dangerous snags — downed trees with gnarled, intact balls of roots that had a nasty habit of lying just below the water's surface. Clark wrote of one such snag near present-day

Top: The river was dredged to deepen the channel, as shown here, near Lower Arago Bend at Holt County in northwest Missouri.
Opposite: Ice floats on the Missouri River, near Columbia.

TAMING THE RIVER

These photos were taken at Indian Cave Bend at Holt County in northwest Missouri.

Top: The Missouri River was once a maze of braided streams that flowed around sandbars and islands. Its water covered nearly 181,000 acres. Lewis and Clark made many references in their journals to the difficulty they had in navigating the dangerous river.

Center: In the early twentieth century, the Army Corps of Engineers altered the river's course by removing snags, dredging the channel, and building wing dikes and piers to direct the current into the center and away from the shoreline.

Bottom: The Corps created a straighter, narrower, and deeper river, without the oxbow curves, dangerous snags, sandbars, and islands that Lewis and Clark saw when they traveled along the river. The water in the Missouri River today covers less than half of the area it once spread over.

Arrow Rock on June 9, 1804: "Sturn of the boat Struck a log which was not proceiveable. ... Struck her bow and turn the boat against Some drift & Snags which [were] below with great force; This was a disagreeable and Dangerous Situation, particularly as immense large trees were Drifting down and we lay imediately in their Course. "

Traveling such a river required various forms of propulsion. Rowing was by far the most common, sails were used to a limited degree, and the men also used poles, which they jammed into the muck to push themselves upriver when rapids threatened the unwieldy boats. Sometimes, the crew resorted to cordelling, in which a sturdy rope was tied to the bow, and the men would get in the river or on the bank to pull the boat along.

A Superhighway for Steamboats

It wasn't long before new technologies took hold on the Missouri, and by 1819, the first steamboat was plying the Big Muddy. Steamboat traffic reached its peak in 1880, when steamboats shipped flour, salt, corn, tobacco, and hemp downriver to St. Louis and beyond and returned with molasses, sugar, coffee, and manufactured items. Rocheport, a mid-Missouri river town, saw fifty-seven steamboats make five hundred landings in 1849 alone. The paddle wheeler's shallow draft eventually allowed river men to travel upriver 2,285 miles from the mouth to Fort Benton, Montana.

The river continued to evolve naturally and, more dramatically, by the hands of man. In a world that covets control and progress, the Missouri River was a wild card. It was moody, erratic, and unpredictable. It crept out of its banks, and it didn't always make things easy for commercial navigation, which had become vital to the opening of the West. So the U.S. Army Corps of Engineers got to work and sculpted a new river where the *Pekitanoui* flowed.

Snags were being removed as early as 1824 to facilitate barge traffic, and Congress appropriated funds specifically for Missouri River improvement beginning in 1881. But it was the Missouri River Bank Stabilization and Navigation Project, which Congress first authorized in 1912, that set the wheels in motion to create a permanent navigation channel from St. Louis to Sioux City, Iowa.

The Corps started by removing hundreds upon hundreds of snags. Then, they removed oxbow bends in the river and straightened the river's course. The Corps accomplished this by building wing dikes and piers into the river to divert the current away from the eroding shoreline. They shored up the banks with rock and dredged the center of the channel, creating an amazingly efficient river — at least nine feet deep in most spots and three hundred yards wide — that rushes by at speeds of four to five miles per hour. It's been called America's fastest navigable river, but today, it's more like a fast-moving drainage ditch than a Garden of Eden.

As much as ninety percent of the biodiversity once found in the river and along its banks is gone. As slow-moving backwaters were removed to create a single channel, important habitat was destroyed. When the river was straitjacketed and confined to a third of its historic flood plain, yearly flooding was disrupted, turning swampy wetlands, which are great for fish, amphibians, reptiles, and insects, into topsoil suitable for farming.

As the Corps of Discovery journeyed across Missouri, the men noted deer in great numbers along the banks "skipping in every derection." Of the diverse creatures noted in the journals in Missouri, many are gone, such as the wild elk and bison, most of the black bear, and the bright green and yellow Carolina parakeets that once ranged from the Canadian border to the Gulf of Mexico and from the Atlantic Ocean to the Rocky Mountains.

But fortunately, much of the scenery and the panoramic views Lewis and Clark beheld can still be seen today. The explorers immediately fell in love with Missouri's lush green valleys, and they recorded that wild roses hugged the riverbanks, along with ripening berries, grapes, and papaws, a fruit they found in abundance along the riverbanks. In their journals, they described the area with reverence: "land verry good ... butifull a peas of land as ever I saw … one of the most beatifull and picteresk seens that I ever beheld. "

On the western edge of Missouri, on July 3, 1804, the party reported seeing the North American beaver for the first time. As the expedition continued west, the men would see countless more. An insatiable fashion craze for beaver hats triggered increased exploration and settlement over the next thirty years, an era often called the golden age of the American fur trade. The fur trade also jumpstarted the growth of a small town called St. Louis.

Although the river was a key factor in American growth, the country's progress quickly outpaced the transportation offered by water. With the growth of railroad shipping in the nineteenth century and commercial trucking in the twentieth century, commerce on the river slowed significantly. Today, more than 1.5 million tons of commodities — primarily fertilizer and grains — are moved by barge annually on the Missouri, which is a drop in the bucket compared to the bustle of traffic on the Mississippi River.

The river also ceased to be a source of mystery or a vital means of information and communication. Now, we seem to have explored and measured all things, from the world's tallest mountain to the black depths of the ocean. Any random search on the internet for "Missouri River" brings up close to a quarter of a million entries. Lewis and Clark's journals were not published for eight years after their return, but visitors to modern-day reenactments on replicas of the Corps of Discovery's boats expect daily photographs and journal updates on the internet.

A Source of Both Debate and Inspiration

After floods in 1993 and 1995 devastated many communities and destroyed thousands of acres of farmland, many state and federal agencies made it a priority to reopen some areas of the river's historic flood plain. The agencies include the U.S. Fish and Wildlife Service,

Limestone bluffs across the state overlook the channel.

Current management allows the river to roam in restored wetlands near Eagle Bluffs Conservation Area south of Columbia.

Big Muddy National Fish and Wildlife Refuge, the Army Corps of Engineers, and the Missouri Department of Conservation.

To date, more than eighty-eight thousand acres of bottomland have been purchased by these agencies to give the river room to breathe and swell, to allow for the growth of newly planted bottomland trees, and to make possible once again that important interchange between land and water: the wetlands. Their efforts also will help to prevent communities from being flooded, protect farms, and preserve and restore lost habitat for fish and wildlife. By not replacing levees that were destroyed during the floods in the 1990s, the Corps of Engineers and the Fish and Wildlife Service have allowed the river to create a shallow side chute near Lisbon, Missouri, north of Boonville. Larval specimens of the endangered pallid sturgeon were collected there in 1998 and 1999. The return of some wetlands has brought on the resurgence of several other endangered species, including the bald eagle.

Still, discussion over the river's future is ongoing. Dams constructed on the upper Missouri River in Montana and the Dakotas collect water that the Corps releases from reservoirs, sending water downriver to Missouri and other states. Recent droughts have led those upper-river states to request that water be held back in the reservoirs to allow recreational boating there. Downriver, however, commercial interests want to see more water released to allow year-round barge traffic. Environmental interests, with yet another perspective, would like to see the Corps release water in a way that mimics the river's natural habit of rising in spring from winter snow melts and dropping in summer and fall to create sandbars and islands for wildlife habitat. And so, the debate rages on.

But, through history, policy changes, and progress, the Missouri River still flows. Once the domain of river men and explorers, the river is now a silent place for the most part, where poets and painters keep watch, and the occasional barge parts the water. According to the Department of Conservation, the river is Missouri's most underused natural water resource. Somehow, the longest river system in the United States manages to meander like a silent blue ribbon across our state, slipping all but unnoticed past more than 4.5 million Missourians who live within a few minutes of it, from St. Joseph to Kansas City to Jefferson City, and on to St. Charles and St. Louis.

Perhaps that's because the beauty of the Missouri River valley is a sublime quality that comes on slowly, as the light shifts and the geese alight. Its beauty lies in its perfect palette of saturated blues and greens, and in its silence. Thousands of cubic feet of river and sediment plow by every minute with the force of a thousand freight trains, yet the river is quieter than a sleeping infant.

In our frontierless age, the Missouri River also offers solace. It's a place where we can reconnect with nature, with our country's past, with the revering gaze of yesterday's explorers, and where we can reconnect with our own wildness. It gives the soul a place to breathe and reserves a space for nature to reign supreme.

On the Big Muddy, whether you look upstream or down, the river appears to stretch to infinity. Some days it is as gray as a city park pigeon on an overcast day. On other days the river is bluer than a baby's eyes. And if you strain your eyes to that distant point on the horizon, the river stretches right up to the limits of land until it kisses the sky, and they dissolve into one. That's what draws the poets, the paddlers, the bird watchers, the hunters, and the fishermen. In our measured world, the river is one of those things that seems to go on forever. It's wild. Relentless. Never-ending.

ABOUT THE AUTHOR: Brett Dufur is the author of several books, including *The Complete Katy Trail Guidebook*. He is the editor and publisher at Pebble Publishing Inc., a publisher of Missouri-related books at Rocheport. He is also the author of the guidebook, *Exploring Lewis & Clark's Missouri*. For more information, visit www.pebblepublishing.com.

Gielomih.

Kishagash.

Minchchatahoch.

S. Coté de Delpech

L. Boilly 1827.

Osages

Peuplade Sauvage de l'Amérique Septentrionale, dans l'État de Missouri

arrivés a Paris le 13. Aout 1827.

WARRIORS OF THE MISSOURI WATERWAYS

By J. Frederick Fausz

WITH THE LOUISIANA PURCHASE in 1803, Americans took notice of the numerous Indian nations living west of the Mississippi River, and three of the main objectives of the Lewis and Clark expedition involved these western Indians. The captains were to announce that the United States now controlled the Indians' territories, begin peaceful diplomatic relations by giving gifts to the Indians, and establish or expand the St. Louis fur trade far up the Missouri River.

Meriwether Lewis and William Clark were based in and around St. Louis for several months before their journey to the Pacific, and while there, they learned that two nearby indigenous Indian nations, the Missouris and the Osages, had played central roles in the development of a distinctive and prosperous culture in Missouri for a century before the explorers' arrival. By the time Lewis and Clark passed through the area, the cultures of the Missouris and the Osages were in decline, but in the years before the captains arrived, both were considered great nations.

The Mighty Missouris

On Wednesday, June 13, 1804, Lewis, Clark, and their Corps of Volunteers for North Western Discovery passed a beautiful prairie and an abandoned village site along the Missouri River near the mouth of the Grand River. The Americans commented that the Missouri Indians who once lived there had been "the real proprietors of an extensive and fertile country" and "the most numerous nation inhabiting the Missouri [River] when first known to the French."

The Missouri tribe, known as the *Peki-tan-oui* by Illinois Algonquians and as the *Ouemessourit* by Father Jacques Marquette and Louis Joliet in 1673, were Chiwere Siouans related to the Winnebago, Oto, and Ioway Indians. They migrated from the Great Lakes to the Lower Missouri River with the Oto and Ioway tribes long before the French arrived in the area.

The Missouris lived in permanent villages where women cultivated maize, beans, and squash, and men hunted animals for food and clothing. Today, Van Meter State Park, near Miami, Missouri, is on a site that was formerly part of the Missouri Indians' homeland.

The Missouri tribe achieved fame and fortune through their deal-

> THE MISSOURI AND OSAGE INDIANS HAD BEEN THE DOMINANT TRIBES IN MISSOURI FOR A CENTURY BEFORE LEWIS AND CLARK'S ARRIVAL

ings with the French-Canadian explorer, soldier, and entrepreneur, Etienne de Veniard, Sieur de Bourgmont, who lived among them from 1714 to 1724. A Missouri woman bore Bourgmont a son, nicknamed Petit Missouri, who accompanied his father and Missouri chiefs and warriors on an ambitious 1724 peace parley with Plains Apaches in south-central Kansas.

Bourgmont and a group of Missouri Indians undertook an even more important diplomatic mission the following year, when they sailed to France, visited Paris and Versailles, and had an audience with King Louis XV at the Chateau de Fontainebleau. French officials considered their friendship and fur trade with the Missouris so important that they gave the Missouri chief gifts, including a musket, a sword, a watch, a medal with a gold chain, and a painting commemorating his meeting with the king. While in France, the chief's daughter was baptized at the Cathedral of Notre Dame and married a French soldier. In 1752, she was living at Kaskaskia and still had her father's Parisian watch.

The Missouris prospered in the southern branch of the French-Canadian fur trade during the first half of the eighteenth century. Fort d'Orleans, a fur outpost that operated near their main village from 1723 to 1728, provided them with the most desirable European trade goods, including muskets, gunpowder, bullet lead, imported flints, iron axes, tomahawks, sharp metal knives, red and blue trade cloth, shirts and other clothing, copper kettles, scissors, brass wire, needles, awls, and items of personal adornment such as colorful glass beads, rings, necklaces, mirrors, combs, hawk's bells, and vermilion, a red mercury sulfide body pigment. When Fort d'Orleans closed in 1728, the Missouris took their deerskins and other furs farther west to Fort de Cavagnial, a new outpost that operated during the 1740s near the present site of Leavenworth, Kansas.

A Drastic Decline

The Missouris' prosperity came at a high price, however, for in only half a century, they were ravaged by smallpox epidemics and the devastating raids of jealous trading rivals. Their exposed Missouri River location made them vulnerable to attacks by the British-allied Sauk and Fox Indians from northern Illinois. In their journals, Lewis and

INDIANS IN MISSOURI

Top: The Sauk and Fox Indians from northern Illinois played a major role in the Missouri Indians' demise. In a journal entry dated June 13, 1804, William Clark described a prairie near the mouth of the Grand River that was once the homeland of the Missouri Indians and noted that it was the "Spot where 300 of them fell a Sacrifise to the fury of the Saukees."

Center: Missouri Indians, left, Otos, center, and Poncas, right, were among the tribes present at the first council Lewis and Clark held with western American Indians August 3, 1804, near the Platte River in what is now northeastern Nebraska.

Bottom: The Oto Indians began moving west from the Mississippi River in the late seventeenth century. The Missouri Indians, who were related to the Oto, joined them in 1798, and the two were essentially regarded as one tribe after that point.

Clark noted that the Sauk and Fox had slaughtered three hundred Missouris in just one raid.

In 1764, as Pierre de Laclede and Auguste Chouteau were constructing a new French fur outpost at St. Louis, the entire Missouri tribe — perhaps six hundred people altogether — arrived in the hopes of settling near the colonial traders. Chouteau recorded his account of the meeting in "Narrative Fragment on the Founding of St. Louis," which was published in John Francis McDermott's *The Early Histories of St. Louis.* "We are like Ducks and Geese," proclaimed the Missouri chief, "worthy of pity and seeking only open water for rest and sustenance." Laclede persuaded them to return to their village to avoid attacks by stronger tribes — "birds of prey" — coming down the Mississippi to "make slaves of your women and children."

With few options left by the 1790s, the decimated Missouris migrated to the Platte River in present-day Nebraska and moved in with their Oto kinsmen. There, Lewis and Clark found the remnants of the once-powerful Missouris in August 1804, when they convened their first meeting with western Indians at Council Bluffs, near what is now the town of Fort Calhoun, Nebraska.

On August 3, 1804, Clark wrote, "Delivered a long Speech to them expressive of our journey the wirkes of our Government, Some advice to them and Directions how They were to Conduct themselves." The captains gave the principal chief a U.S. flag, a large Jefferson peace medal, and some clothes, while smaller silver medals were bestowed on lesser chiefs — three Missouris and three Otos. This first council between the explorers and western Indians ended with an exchange of gifts — gunpowder and whiskey for the Indians, and watermelons for the Corps of Discovery.

The Rise of the Osages

The dramatic decline of the Missouris allowed the Osage Indians to enjoy a golden age of trade and territorial dominance in what is now the state of Missouri between 1764 and 1804. Designated the "great nation south of the Missouri" by Thomas Jefferson, the Osages, or *Ni-U-Kon-Ska,* which means "Children of the Middle Waters," were Dheghian Siouans who had migrated into Missouri from the Ohio Valley with their Quapaw (Arkansas), Kansa, Maha (Omaha), and Ponca kin.

The Osages were divided into two branches — the Grand or Big Osages and the Petit or Little Osages. The Grand Osages built defensible hilltop villages of huge thatched longhouses along the headwaters of the Osage River in what is now Vernon County in far western Missouri. Two physical features of the area were particularly revered by the Grand Osages — Marais des Cygnes, or "Marsh of Swans," and the Blue Mound nearby, which served as a sacred burial site for chiefs. The Osage Village State Historic Site near Nevada, Missouri, commemorates a major agricultural settlement inhabited by Osages for an entire century.

The less populous Little Osages lived near the Missouri tribe for a time but later relocated closer to the Grand Osages for greater secu-

AN UNRIVALED SUPPLY OF FLINTLOCK MUSKETS MADE THE OSAGE THE SCOURGE OF THE CENTRAL PRAIRIES

rity from raids. Near the end of the eighteenth century, a third group, the Arkansas or Southern Osages, split from the Grand Osages and relocated to the northeastern corner of present-day Oklahoma because of political factionalism and the abundance of game animals in that region.

The Osages exploited their strategic location midway between the Mississippi River and the Great Plains and between Canada and New Orleans to become Missouri's greatest Indian traders since the Cahokian civilization collapsed four centuries earlier. The hunter-warriors of the Osages harvested the animals most desired by fur traders across three distinct ecological zones, from the bison on the plains to the deer in the forests to the bears of the Ozark Mountains. As early as 1717, French traders praised the Osages as the best fur producers south of Canada, primarily because talented Osage women actually manufactured exquisitely brain-tanned and shaved deer leather from the raw skins that their husbands harvested. Brain tanning is a process that uses deer, elk, or bison brain and human urine to cure animal hides and create a soft, supple, light-colored leather.

The European fur trade centered in St. Louis provided the Osages with all of the imported luxuries earlier enjoyed by the Missouris, but the unrivaled supply of flintlock muskets made the two thousand or so Osage warriors the scourge of the central prairies, which encompassed about one hundred thousand square miles from the banks of the Mississippi to the Great Plains and from Iowa into central Arkansas and Oklahoma. Described by some as resembling ancient Romans or medieval knights, the Osage warriors were, according to President Jefferson, gigantic men, usually exceeding six feet in height. They scraped or burned off much of their hair, leaving only a small tuft on top of the head and a scalplock hanging down the back. It must have been quite a spectacle to see hundreds of these red-painted, nearly bald warriors riding their war ponies at full gallop and armed with long, lethal lances, French flintlock muskets, scalping knives, and their famous bows made of Osage orangewood, or *bois d'arc.*

However, despite their fierce reputation, the Osages were the trusted allies of the powerful Chouteau family of St. Louis, doubly bound to them through bloodlines as well as business ties. The Osage traded heavily with the Chouteau family, and young Chouteau men often took a liking to Osage women, resulting in familial bonds between the two groups. In a rare convergence of mutual interest and intercultural understanding, the Chouteaus and the Osages prospered together and shared common fears of hostile Indians loyal to the British and expanding American settlements east of the Mississippi River.

The Osages, despite being dreaded by tribal enemies and Spanish officials for their dominance in the fur trade, were the foundation of St. Louis's peace and prosperity for four decades. Their dressed deerskins, often called "bucks," were the main currency used throughout the colonial settlements of eastern Missouri. A visiting Frenchman once described them as the real bankers of the region. Moreover, they supplied one-half or more of the precious furs — measured by volume as well as value — that made St. Louis a successful and affluent regional capital of worldwide commerce, even though the town had fewer than fifteen hundred white residents.

The End of an Era

Despite their prosperity, the decade before the Louisiana Purchase was a turbulent one for the Osages. The fur trade had put a strain on the area's animal resources, and after the Chickasaws killed three prominent Osage chiefs on the lower Mississippi River in 1794, political rivalries and commercial realities forced nearly half of the Grand Osages to move south. The remaining Osages in Missouri faced new rivals — hundreds of Shawnee and Delaware warriors who had been invited to relocate from the Ohio Valley to the Cape Girardeau area by Spanish officials who wanted to intimidate the insolent, militarily dominant Osages. War with those Algonquian mercenaries was averted when the Chouteaus built Fort Carondelet near Marais des Cygnes, providing the Osages with essential supplies and weapons so that they would not have to raid white settlements along the Mississippi for provisions.

While rival St. Louis merchants, jealous of the lucrative Chouteau-Osage trade monopoly, sponsored several expeditions far up the Missouri River in the mid-1790s to search for alternative sources of furs, all of the residents of the Louisiana Purchase territory — Indians, French, and Spanish alike — feared that an American invasion of their lands was imminent. Even though the American "invasion" occurred peacefully through purchase rather than military conquest, the end result was the same for the Osages. The valuable knowledge they had imparted to their French trading partners about the people and places in the West was critically important to the success of Lewis and Clark's expedition in particular and to American territorial governance in general.

However, the Osages' worst fears were realized when Lewis and Clark returned from the Pacific Ocean. The captains became senior officials in the trans-Mississippi West and systematically cleared Missouri of its Indians to make way for thousands of American settlers. Once the Corps of Discovery located the rich fur resources of the northern plains, the Osages became expendable as animal harvesters and trade allies. Although the Osages never warred against the United States, Lewis and Clark dispossessed them of fifty thousand square miles of territory in the 1808 Treaty of Fort Osage and relocated them to a sliver of land in the western part of the state, a tiny slice of their once-massive Missouri homeland. Once the precious territory of the Osages became more coveted than their profitable trade by Americans seeking fertile farmlands, the long chapter of Missouri history dominated by Indian relations came to an end.

Because the descendants of the Missouri and Osage Indians have

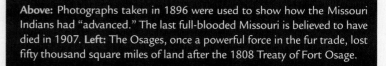

Above: Photographs taken in 1896 were used to show how the Missouri Indians had "advanced." The last full-blooded Missouri is believed to have died in 1907. **Left:** The Osages, once a powerful force in the fur trade, lost fifty thousand square miles of land after the 1808 Treaty of Fort Osage.

spent the past 130 years living in Oklahoma, many of today's citizens do not realize the significant role those native nations played in Missouri's early development. The intercultural cooperation and toleration that marked the French and Indian fur trade in the eighteenth century was quickly abandoned by American policies after the Louisiana Purchase and was never revived.

As Nicolas de Finiels, a French visitor to Missouri and Illinois, wrote in 1803: The French colonists generated a unique "affection … in the hearts of all the Indian nations," while "the English, Anglo-American, and Spanish nations have succeeded only in inspiring fear and alienation." He went on to lament the fact that "Louisiana's adolescence was the most felicitous time that the region has experienced thus far."

ABOUT THE AUTHOR: J. Frederick Fausz is a history professor at the University of Missouri-St. Louis who specializes in the ethnohistory of American Indians and the American fur trade from the seventeenth century to the early nineteenth century.

TRADING TRADITIONS

By J. Frederick Fausz

IN EARLY 1764, a small band of ambitious New Orleans entrepreneurs, led by French-born gentleman-merchant Pierre de Laclede and his precocious fourteen-year-old stepson, Auguste Chouteau, founded St. Louis, France's last officially authorized fur outpost in North America. As the heir to a long and lucrative Canadian commercial heritage, the tiny village would ultimately become "one of the finest cities in America," as Laclede predicted, by uniting a few hundred Europeans with several thousand Indians as partners in the quest for animal skins for international markets from Europe to China. The French-dominated fur trade of St. Louis was the single greatest influence on the development of early Missouri in the four decades before the Louisiana Purchase, and its tangible legacies can still be found throughout our state today.

St. Louis's spectacular rise to prominence was due to its ideal location, impeccable timing, and enduring traditions of interethnic cooperation and tolerance for native cultures. Perched atop a limestone bluff, St. Louis was strategically situated near the confluence of America's two longest rivers with the greatest commercial potential. This new trading center at the crossroads of the continent was created just after France had surrendered its vast Canadian and Great Lakes empire to Great Britain in the 1763 Treaty of Paris. Laclede's settlement immediately became a magnet of French culture that attracted long-established Catholic fur merchants from southern Illinois who did not wish to live under the Union Jack. Since France had also transferred its vast trans-Mississippi territories to the loose control of Spain in 1762, St. Louis residents found themselves in an ideal position to exploit the unrivaled fur resources of "soft gold" in the far west.

The insatiable demand in Europe and Asia for furs from animals that had long been extinct outside of North America could only be satisfied by the hunting and processing skills of American Indians, who monopolized the supply of mammals from their extensive and jealously guarded territories. The early fur trade had always been an "Indian trade," and the survival and success of St. Louis depended upon a cooperative alliance between natives and newcomers. Laclede's outpost was fortunate in attracting experienced, enlightened merchants, interpreters, and voyageurs (boatmen) from Montreal, Quebec, and older French settlements throughout Illinois and Louisiana. These creoles, or French-speakers born in America, already respected the different traditions and vital contributions of Indians.

> WHEN THOMAS JEFFERSON PURCHASED THE LOUISIANA TERRITORY IN 1803, ST. LOUIS BECAME THE COUNTRY'S CAPITAL OF THE WESTERN FUR TRADE

Osage Partners

The most important of St. Louis's Indian pelt partners were the Osages, the largest and most powerful tribe south of the Missouri River. Their soft, shaved, and brain-tanned deerskins were world-famous long before 1764 and served as the main currency ("bucks") in St. Louis well into the American period. By extensively harvesting and expertly processing a variety of skins, hides, and pelts, from the largest bison to the smallest weasel, the Osages provided at least half of all furs exported from St. Louis in the eighteenth century.

During St. Louis's first decade, the founding Laclede-Chouteau family maintained its position of preeminence by amassing one hundred thousand to three hundred thousand pounds of furs per year from the Osages and half a dozen other tribes in the Missouri River basin. In 1778, after Laclede's premature death at age forty-eight from natural causes, his heirs, Auguste and Pierre Chouteau, strengthened the Osage business alliance with blood ties, fathering children with Osage women (with public baptisms in St. Louis's downtown cathedral), and participating in tribal councils. The Chouteaus and their European marriage partners formed a monopolistic oligarchy but never forgot that the Osages were the most important source of peace and prosperity in "Chouteau's Town," as St. Louis was known to its many Indian allies.

Expensive gift-giving and elaborate diplomatic hospitality were important for maintaining the friendship of area tribes, and every year dozens of Indian delegations arrived at St. Louis to be wined and dined and otherwise rewarded for their critical support of the eighteenth-century Missouri fur trade. Imported products of cloth, glass, and metal were the staples of the Indian trade, but weapons became increasingly important in the 1790s, as the Osages struggled to defend their one-hundred-thousand-square-mile animal empire, upon which the wealth and security of St. Louis depended. In that decade, the Chouteau brothers built Fort Carondelet in far-western Missouri as an exclusive Osage trading post.

At the same time, they armed their Indian friends and relatives with dozens of muskets, ten thousand European gunflints, several tons of bullet lead, large quantities of gunpowder, seventeen hundred "scalping knives," and one thousand pounds of vermilion, the red powder the Indians favored as war paint.

"Guns and knives were absolutely essential [to the] Missouri trade,"

The eighteenth-century fur trade created a high demand for guns and ammunition. This Indian trade musket from the 1790s, antique powder horn, and lead musket balls may have belonged to fur traders.

Auguste Chouteau wrote in the 1790s, because "all the tribes on the Mississippi have declared war" on the Osages, who possessed "the only land nowadays that still has game."

While the Osages defended hunting grounds from rival European and Indian poachers in often lethal encounters, French voyageurs retrieved other furs from as far as one thousand miles up the Missouri River and deposited them in warehouses along the St. Louis waterfront. From there, cargoes of heavy buffalo hides and deerskins were sent down the Mississippi to New Orleans on flatboats, while delicate "peltries" (lynxes, foxes, martens, ermines, et cetera), beaver pelts, and other furs that could not tolerate heat and high humidity were wrapped in Ozark bearskins and transported by huge bark canoes up the Illinois River and across Lake Michigan to the great trade mart at Michilimackinac. Since boat travel upriver from New Orleans was dangerous and tedious — often taking longer than a trans-Atlantic voyage — St. Louis received most of its trade merchandise through Montreal and Michilimackinac, with bark canoes returning down the Mississippi by way of Green Bay.

Luxurious Living

The St. Louis furs that were sold in Montreal and London coffeehouse auctions paid for a wealth of merchandise, both practical and exotic, from around the world. The quantity and quality of European products that flowed into St. Louis from Canada gave Missouri's small white population one of the highest standards of living on any North American frontier. In single shipments during the 1790s, the Chouteau brothers alone imported seventy-two pounds of licorice, fifty pounds of chocolate, sixteen pounds of peppermint, two hundred pounds of South American coffee, and one ton of Canadian maple syrup, as well as Caribbean sugar, Chinese tea, Asian spices, European patent medicines, and tobacco from several regions. In addition to tons of tools, kitchenware, and more practical consumer goods, St. Louis voyageurs also brought back baguettes and biscuits from Montreal bakeries, premium hams, kegs of rum, the finest Madeira wine, fourteen-foot virgin wool point blankets from the best looms of England, linen, lace, silk, muslin, cotton, and canvas from several countries, and even brand name cloth products, such as

FUR TRADE RENDEZVOUS

William Ashley of the Rocky Mountain Fur Company established the fur trade rendezvous system in 1825 in present-day Wyoming. Fur trappers and traders would gather to exchange money, trade goods, and supplies from St. Louis for the furs trapped in the Rocky Mountains. Each rendezvous was also a social event, where the men could sing, dance, play games, and celebrate before heading back to their trapping grounds. The rendezvous period lasted only until 1840, but numerous events designed to replicate the rendezvous are scheduled throughout the year in Missouri.

Flatlanders who visit these modern-day events have the opportunity to experience the past with all five senses: they can taste some buffalo stew; see buckskinners as they perform period tasks from building birch bark canoes to patching moccasins; hear bagpipes, fifes, and tin whistles; smell the scents of leather, black powder, and wood smoke that fill the air; and feel first-hand the coarseness of the outer, protective guard hairs on a beaver pelt or the silky soft-

ness of a silver fox's fur.

The rendezvous today is a family affair, and many events, demonstrations, and competitions are designed to entertain and educate, including tomahawk and knife throwing, muzzleloading rifle shooting, cannon drills, costume exhibitions, and period melodrama performances. The modern rendezvous ranges in size from local events with a dozen camps to national gatherings with several hundred camps.

Some rendezvous events in Missouri:

December 31, 2003 to January 4, 2004
Sarcoxie
Medicine Winter Muzzleloaders Family Rendezvous
417-548-2629

April 10-11, 2004
Greenville
26th Annual Old Greenville Black Powder Rendezvous
573-624-6290

May 1-2, 2004
Hermitage
18th Annual Pomme de Terre Rendezvous
417-745-2362

May 14-23, 2004
St. Charles
Lewis and Clark Heritage Days
636-946-7776

September 18-19, 2004
St. Louis
Fort Bellefontaine Historic Encampment
314-544-5714

October 2-3, 2004
Bloomfield
5th Annual Crowley's Ridge Black Powder Rendezvous
715-866-8890

Note: *Many of these events are held every year on corresponding dates, although contact information might change.*

—Erwin Neighbors

"Alton Thread" and "Illinois Kerchiefs #23."

Thanks to the fur trade, St. Louis families could purchase expensive Moroccan leather shoes, tailored clothing, silver jewelry, and even white gloves for all ages. In 1794, Pierre Chouteau treated himself to an exquisite, name-brand "Sam Beazley" London saddle, with rivets, stirrups, and the initials "PC" all rendered in fine silver. In addition to the weapons and war paint mentioned earlier, Indian allies received luxury items imported through Canada, including 150,000 French porcelain beads and 270 black silk handkerchiefs in one shipment!

The lavish entertaining enjoyed by Meriwether Lewis, William Clark, and even the Marquis de Lafayette at the beautiful mansions of the urbane Chouteau brothers represented the lifestyles of the rich and famous fur merchants in boomtown Missouri. Villages with self-deprecating nicknames — translated as Short of Bread (St. Louis), Misery (Ste. Genevieve), and Empty Pockets (Carondelet) — were misleading with regard to the actual prosperity enjoyed by many French creoles in Upper Louisiana. While St. Louis residents concentrated on trade rather than agriculture, surrounding communities fed them in exchange for desirable imported merchandise that only the furs could purchase. Radiating from the hub of St. Louis like the spokes of a wheel, the nearby villages of Cahokia, Prairie du Rocher, Kaskaskia, Carondelet, Florissant, St. Charles, and Ste. Genevieve formed an integrated network of complementary economic specialties. Statistics for 1803 reveal that Upper Louisiana (eastern Missouri and southern Illinois) had a population of four thousand people, both free and slave, producing 27,000 bushels of wheat, 33,000 bushels of maize, 22,000 pounds of tobacco, 120,000 pounds of lead, 4,200 bushels of salt, and enough fodder to feed 4,600 cattle and 815 horses.

The same year, the fur harvest reached a new low, but gross returns of almost seventy-eight thousand dollars and profits of 70 percent still made it an important part of regional prosperity. (See "Partial Fur Harvest-St. Louis," page 30.)

The diversified economy of eastern Missouri, based upon fur trade profits from global commerce as well as local farms, mines, and salt works, proved almost as alluring as New Orleans for Americans with an interest in the Louisiana Territory. The U.S. acquisition of St. Louis, in fact, provided the earliest dividends to the American nation, as French merchants and loyal Indian allies assisted Lewis and Clark with invaluable information about the lower sixteen hundred miles of the Missouri River, while fur trade voyageurs and interpreters actually joined the Corps of Discovery.

Cultural Center

By every measure, the St. Louis fur trade was an unqualified success and a climactic tribute to the French colonial heritage. The Gateway City enriched the economies of older creole villages and founded several new satellite outposts throughout the central prairie-plains, including the earliest settlements at Kansas City and St. Joseph. The St. Louis fur trade pioneered new methods of animal harvesting in the far west up to the Civil War and continued to be a major player in international fur trading well into the twentieth century, ending as a leading processor of Alaskan sealskins. As the meeting ground of many cultures, St. Louis also became a leading center of knowledge about the peoples, places, and products of the American West — a legacy that lives on in civic institutions, such as the Mercantile Library (now based at the University of Missouri-St. Louis), Missouri

Above: Beads, bells, and cloth items — and whiskey to a lesser extent — were popular trade items in eighteenth-century Missouri. Sky-blue beads were favorite gifts during the Lewis and Clark expedition. **Bottom:** This beaver hat, shown with a red fox pelt , dates back to the 1830s.

Above: Antique trade axes from England, France, and Spain were used to arm Indian fur allies throughout the Mississippi and Missouri river valleys. The shiny ax in the center dates to about 1800 and is of a rare design that was popular among the Osage Indians.

Historical Society, Saint Louis Art Museum, and Missouri Botanical Garden. Many residents and tourists visit those institutions to learn more about the fascinating fur trade of a bygone era, while modern maps of Missouri still record the names of traders and tribes that made the state's first industry famous the world over.

Often overlooked, however, is how the arrival of Americans in 1804 revolutionized the old French commercial heritage. The United States quickly changed things for all Missouri residents, beginning as soon as Lewis and Clark returned to St. Louis in 1806. The rich reserves of beaver and bison they discovered far upriver encouraged white and black trappers — the "Mountain Men" — to exploit the Indians' animal resources themselves, without sharing the profits. With their influence and market share greatly reduced, the loyal Osages became expendable. Between 1808 and 1825, St. Louis's oldest Indian allies were forced out of the Missouri that they had helped create when their vast territory became more coveted for farms than for furs.

While Missouri's French population adapted fairly quickly to a new flag, new government, new economy, and new language following the Louisiana Purchase, long-term American policies made many Indians lament the change in administration. Never again would the leading citizens of St. Louis be so accepting of the Indians' different cultures and worldviews. Trading traditions during the French colonial period made Missouri a model of cultural toleration by placing human relationships at the core of Western discovery.

ABOUT THE AUTHOR: **J. Frederick Fausz** is a history professor at the University of Missouri-St. Louis who specializes in the ethnohistory of American Indians and the American fur trade from the seventeenth century to the early nineteenth century.

PARTIAL FUR HARVEST — ST. LOUIS, 1804

Dressed Deerskins (shaved and tanned)	97,000 lbs @ .40 /lb	$38,800
"Red" Deerskins "in the hair"	6,400 lbs @ .50 /lb	$3,200
Beaver Pelts	12,300 lbs @ 1.20/lb	$14,800
Bison Hides & Robes	1,700 lbs @ 3.00/lb	$5,100
Ozark Black Bearskins	2,500 lbs @ 2.00/lb	$5,000
Otter Pelts	1,300 lbs @ 4.00/lb	$5,000
Raccoon Skins	4,200 lbs @ .25/lb	$1,000
Fox Pelts	800 lbs @ .50/lb	$400
Animal Tallow	8,300 lbs @ .20/lb	$1,700
Bear Grease	2,300 gals @ 1.20/gal	$2,600

Source: Data from Zadok Cramer, The Navigator, 8th ed. (Pittsburgh: Robert Ferguson & Co., Printers, 1814), 342-343

This Osage warrior is wearing handkerchiefs, vermilion body paint, beads, a silver brooch, and an armband that were all imported from Canada by the Chouteaus. The warrior was part of an Osage delegation that visited President Jefferson in 1804.

"the last settlement of whites on this river..."

—from the journal of the Corps of Discovery's Sgt. Charles Floyd

By Lowell M. Schake

WHEN THE UNITED STATES acquired the Louisiana Purchase in 1803, two-thirds of its citizens resided near the Atlantic Coast. Only four roads crossed the Alleghenies, and the United States did not extend beyond the Mississippi River. To the west of this boundary stretched a vast wilderness, mysterious and unknown except to a few trappers, squatters, and fur traders on the Missouri River. For Europeans and Americans, the gateway to this wilderness was a tiny village called La Charrette, which once stood near present-day Marthasville.

The name of the village and of a creek near the site came from an event in the late eighteenth century. In 1795, Jean Baptiste Trudeau, leader of the Missouri Trading Company for the Discovery of the Nations of the Upper Missouri wrote in his journal, "On the tenth of July, I unfortunately lost one of my Frenchmen, named Joseph Chorette, who was drowned while bathing alone at dusk, in the Missouri."

Trudeau's crew, local squatters, and American Indian children and adults searched for Chorette for days while Trudeau traded furs. Chorette was forever lost to the river, but in his honor, nearby Wolf Creek was named Chorette's Creek. The presence of two-wheeled French carts, known as *charettes,* may have influenced the change from *Chorette* to *Charrette.* Documents from the early 1800s include both spellings. Lewis and Clark misspelled the creek as *Chouritte* in their journals and spelled the name of the village as *Charatt, Charette,* and *Chirotte* in references to the settlement.

Joseph Chartran was fifty-nine years old when he founded the village of La Charrette in 1801. Chartran was known as the Ancient Syndic, a term that referred to his role as official or magistrate. Although there is no documented evidence of an established trading post on the site before this time, squatters and fur traders had been active in the area since 1769 and perhaps earlier. Under a 1798 Spanish law, larger families were entitled to larger land claims. Chartran had adopted five orphans by the time he settled at La Charrette, and several other families who settled the area had taken in orphans as well. The orphans might have come from St. Louis or

> WHEN LEWIS AND CLARK SET OUT FOR THE WEST, THE LAST WHITE SETTLEMENT THEY ENCOUNTERED WAS LA CHARRETTE, NEAR PRESENT-DAY MARTHASVILLE

St. Charles, but their heritage is unknown. Historic records make no further mention of them.

Within a few years, the fur-trapping families began leaving the area. Their Spanish land grants were denied after the Louisiana Purchase was transferred from Spain to France to the United States. Next, black slaves owned by relatives of Rebecca and Daniel Boone cultivated the land. The Boones arrived at nearby Femme Osage in 1799, but family descendants continued to live at La Charrette for three more generations. In the book *Daniel Boone, the Life and Legend of an American Pioneer,* Yale professor of American history John Mack Faragher writes: "By the time the United States acquired Louisiana, Charrette had become a thoroughly mixed village of backcountry Americans, French-speaking Creoles, emigrant and native Indians, free and enslaved African Americans, and a growing progeny of their various combinations."

The People and Their Village

A wide, forested flood plain accented with tall limestone bluffs and rolling hills greeted explorers and traders who docked at La Charrette. Many noted the natural beauty of the region and extolled it as a hunter's paradise. Family traditions in the fur trade and a lifetime of advancing from one frontier to the next compelled the seven adventuresome families of La Charrette to establish a village here.

The family of Jean Marie Cardinal and his Omaha wife, Angelique, were among the original squatters at Charrette Bottoms, which later became La Charrette. According to a genealogy of the Cardinal family, several generations before, Jean Marie's Canadian patriarch Jacques Cardinal was the first to come down the Wisconsin River and trade furs at Ottawa in 1683. Jean Marie established Prairie du Chien in Wisconsin around 1754. During the winter of 1762-63, he and his partner Jose Tebeau became involved in a dispute with two New York fur traders. Jean Marie and Jose killed the men about twenty miles from Prairie du Chien and then fled to St. Charles on the Missouri River to avoid prosecution.

Jean Marie was granted a license to trade furs with the Osages in the district of St. Charles in 1777. His son, Jean Marie Cardinal Jr.,

ding Post

Joseph Chartran

Charles & Cecilia Tayon, Jr.

Jean & Elizabeth Cardinal, Jr.

William & Frances Lamme

M. Ochonicky

Missouri River

also married an American Indian woman and settled at La Charrette with his brother Paul. Other French-Canadian villagers included founder Joseph Chartran, his Osage wife, a son, and five orphans in his care; Jean Baptiste Luzon, his wife, their child, and four orphans; the slave-holding family of Charles Tayon Jr.; Joseph Arnow, Jack Amos, and Madame Louis St. Franceway, who was a widow with one child.

Charles "Indian" Phillips, a displaced Shawnee and friend of Daniel Boone, frequented the village and was a well-known trapper, hunter, and hunting guide. He and other American Indians interacted regularly with the village. Fighting between tribes was common at the time, and some nearby tribes, such as the Potawatomi, Oto, and Fox Indians, sought to challenge the Osages, because the Osages tended to accommodate whites more than other tribes. In 1805, the Frankfort, Kentucky, *Palladium* newspaper reported that four hundred Sacs crossed at La Charrette in May intent on settling a score with the Osages.

In 1806, President Jefferson ordered Capt. Zebulon Pike to provide safe escort to fifty-one ransomed Osage, Oto, and Pawnee Indians who had been captured by the Potawatomis. Eight chiefs of various tribes, who had just returned from a meeting with Jefferson in Washington, D.C., accompanied Pike's group. The Indians walked along the riverbanks singing songs of mourning for family members who had been killed while they had been held captive. Pike traveled upriver by boat as he escorted the Indians to villages along the Missouri River and beyond, all the way to what is now Kansas. The group raised the village population to about seventy-five during its three-day stopover at La Charrette.

Pike stayed in Chartran's French style *bousillage* cabin, which was constructed with vertical logs. Its post-in-ground walls were sealed with a mud and grass mixture, and similar one- or two-room cabins featured dirt floors, open fireplaces, sleeping lofts, one or two small, uncovered windows, and porches in the front and the back. The village spanned eight-tenths of a mile at the water's edge, and a 550-foot-wide strip of land connected each farm on the outlying land to the village at the riverbank. Each farm was about nine hundred arpents, a French unit of measure equal to a little less than an acre.

Most of the farmers tended their gardens and tobacco plants better than their crop fields, as much of their livelihood came from trapping beavers rather than from selling crops. Scrub livestock ran free and ate native grasses, rushes, and then tree bark to survive the cold winters. Hunting dogs, guns, canoes, traps, horses, and firewood were essentials to this frontier community. Barter with maple syrup, beeswax, and beaver pelts was common. For fun, the villagers drank, gambled, and danced at their little trading post.

Lewis and Clark's Arrival

When Lewis and Clark were preparing for their journey, little was known about the American West. At the time, the largest district in the area was St. Charles, which had fewer than four hundred citizens. One-tenth of them lived at La Charrette.

According to the 1975 publication *Lewis and Clark*, by R.G.

ON ITS RETURN TRIP, THE CORPS OF DISCOVERY CHEERED AT THE FAMILIAR SITE OF LA CHARRETTE

Ferris and published by the U.S. Department of the Interior, the explorers would have preferred to spend the winter of 1803-04 at La Charrette. In late 1803, the French denied them permission to proceed west onto the Missouri River until sovereignty over the Louisiana Purchase was officially transferred, so the men spent the winter at Wood River, Illinois, instead.

By May 24, the explorers arrived at Femme Osage Creek with their overloaded flotilla of one keelboat and two pirogues. Captain Clark recorded their May 25, 1804, arrival at La Charrette:

"Camped at the mouth of a Creek called River a Chauritte above a Small french Village of 7 houses and as many families, Settled at this place to be convt. to hunt, & trade with the Indians, here we met with Mr. Louisell imedeately down from the Seeder Isld. ... he informed us that he Saw no Indians on the river below the Poncrars. Some hard rain this evening. The people at this Village is pore, houses Small, they Sent us milk & eggs to eat."

At the village, Lewis was able to gain intelligence about the lands ahead that he had not been able to get during the winter at St. Louis.

One fur trader with extensive experience on the upper Missouri River had been particularly recalcitrant. Manuel Lisa, who was described as "half French, half Spanish, and half grinning alligator," was reluctant to share his knowledge with Lewis. He also purchased the entire inventory of ten-gallon kegs in St. Louis only days before Lewis and Clark were to provision their expedition. Lewis was outraged. In a letter to Clark, he wrote, "Damm Manuel, and triply Damm Mr. B [Lisa's partner]. They give me more vexation than their lives are worth."

But at La Charrette, the Corps of Discovery encountered Regis Loisel, a French-Canadian fur trader who had stopped at the village on his way downriver from Cedar Island. Loisel was an authority on Missouri River geography as far as the Teton River, and Lewis questioned him extensively during the evening they spent at La Charrette. Loisel was able to provide much of the information that Lisa had stubbornly denied the captains at St. Louis. After spending the night at La Charrette, Lewis, Clark, and their crew woke at dawn the next morning and proceeded upriver.

Lewis and Clark's Return

In the late summer of 1806, the Corps of Discovery was making excellent progress on their return trip after traveling all the way to the Pacific Ocean. The men were in a hurry to return home and were reluctant to take the time to hunt for game. Instead, as they came downriver, they took advantage of the readily available papaws, fruits that grow on trees on the rich soil along the Missouri River. Papaws look and taste like relatives to the banana, but they can cause allergic reactions in some people. On September 18, 1806, Clark wrote that the men "appear perfectly contented and tell us that they can live very well on the pappaws."

The next day Clark writes, "Three of the party have their eyes inflamed and Sweled in Such a manner as to render them extreamly painfull, particularly when exposed to the light, the eye ball is much inflaimed and the lid appears burnt with the Sun ..."

The Marthasville Chamber of Commerce is offering numbered medallions to celebrate the bicentennial anniversary of the Corps of Discovery's arrival there May 25, 1804. The medallions cost twenty dollars. To order, call 636-433-5242.

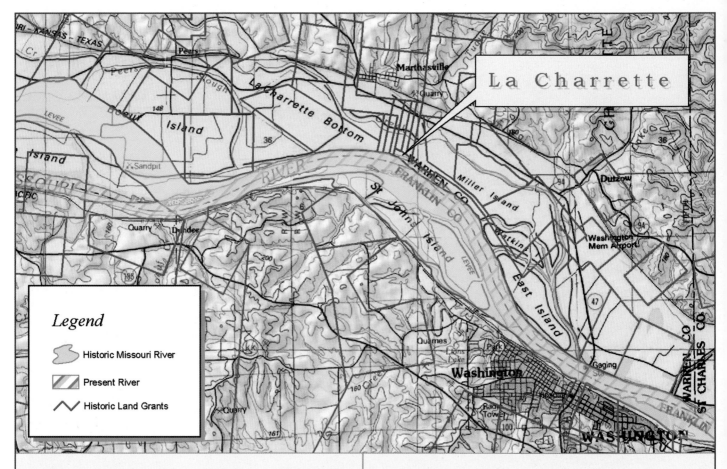

Legend

Historic Missouri River

Present River

Historic Land Grants

On the next day, September 20, 1806, hot and humid weather added to the men's discomfort. The crew's provisions were almost exhausted as, near sunset, they rounded Charrette Bend and saw the familiar village on the north bank of the Missouri River. In his journal entry for that day, Clark wrote:

"The party, being extremely anxious to get down, ply their ors very well. We saw some cows on the bank, which was a joyful sight to the party and caused a shout to be raised for joy. … we came in sight of the little French village called Charrette. The men raised a shout and sprang upon their oars, and we soon landed opposite the village. We landed and were politely received. … We purchased of a citizen two gallons of whiskey for our part, for which we were obliged to give eight dollars cash, an imposition on part of the citizen. … Every person, both French and Americans, seemed to express great pleasure at our return. … They informed us that we were supposed to have been long lost since."

At La Charrette, the men celebrated their return as best they could, even though several still had tearful, swollen eyes.

After the Voyage

A school was established at La Charrette in 1807, but by then, the original French-Canadian families had departed. Many of the original families settled at a new western frontier village, Cote sans Dessein, near the mouth of the Osage River and present-day Tebbetts, about fifty miles west of La Charrette. A new group of slave-holding settlers then inhabited La Charrette, and Nathan Boone, son of Rebecca and Daniel, led the construction of Callaway's Fort there to protect the new village inhabitants from American Indians during the War of 1812. Indians had maintained good relations with the first generation of La Charrette inhabitants,

but by the time the second wave of villagers had settled there, American treatment of the tribes had created animosity.

At least three Corps of Discovery members remained in contact with La Charrette. Clark, who became the Upper Louisiana Territory's agent of Indian affairs and later the first governor of the Missouri Territory, visited La Charrette after negotiating an Osage treaty in 1808. Corps of Discovery member John Colter returned to the area in 1810, married an Indian woman named Sarah, and bought a farm across the river from La Charrette. Robert Frazer, another Corps member, was his neighbor. Both men frequented the village, and Colter died in the area in 1813.

La Charrette was the site of the 1820 funeral of part-time resident Daniel Boone, and a few years later, the settlement fades from history. The village landing was renamed for the larger nearby town of Marthasville, and German settlers who moved into Missouri between 1830 and 1850 began farming the land that was once the site of La Charrette. Today, the village site is on private farmland.

Locally, the place name Charrette lives on with Charrette Creek, Charrette Bottoms, and Charrette Township. The journals of the Corps of Discovery are some of the few remaining bits of evidence of what expedition member Charles Floyd called "the last settlement of whites on this river…"

ABOUT THE AUTHOR: Lowell M. Schake is a retired professor of animal science who lives at Padre Isles, Corpus Christi, Texas. He was born on Charrette Creek, where his ancestors once owned farms at La Charrette. He is the author of the first book to be written about the village, *La Charrette: Village Gateway to the American West,* recently published by iUniverse. Visit www.iuniverse.com to order a copy for $19.95.

A FEW STOUT, HEALTHY MEN

By Ann Rogers

WHEN THE Lewis and Clark expedition moved across what is now Missouri in the summer of 1804, the party comprised forty-seven men, far more than the two figures depicted on historical markers. The number was fourfold the "ten or twelve chosen men" President Jefferson mentioned in a confidential message to Congress in January 1803, when he requested twenty-five hundred dollars for an exploration of the Northwest. From the time he made this request, the number of recruits grew over a period of sixteen months and along fourteen hundred miles of rivers until the expedition's boats began moving up the Missouri River.

Jefferson chose as leader of the expedition twenty-six-year-old Meriwether Lewis, an army captain and fellow Virginian who had been the president's secretary and aide for two years. Lewis in turn invited William Clark to share the command. A Virginian by birth, Clark was four years older than Lewis and had once been commander of an elite rifle company in which Lewis had served. The two men had similar backgrounds and complementary personalities and skills. Throughout the journey, Lewis would often choose to walk along the shore, accompanied only by his Newfoundland dog, and observe plants and animals he would later describe in meticulous detail. Clark would usually remain with the boat crews, mapping with amazing accuracy the rivers they traveled.

Even before the expedition began, the two men demonstrated their ability to work together as an effective team. Lewis wrote to Clark, who was then living at the Falls of the Ohio, near present-day Louisville, Kentucky, and asked him to find "some good hunters, stout, healthy, unmarried men, accustomed to the woods." Clark's candidates included Joseph and Reubin

HOW LEWIS AND CLARK ASSEMBLED THE CREW FOR AMERICA'S MOST SUCCESSFUL MILITARY EXPEDITION

Top: Reenactors from the Discovery Expedition of St. Charles travel past Rocheport in replica pirogues. **Bottom:** Reenactor David Cain, of Kansas City, enjoys the last light of day on the river. **Opposite:** Reenactor Jim Rascher, of St. Louis, scans the river ahead for floating debris.

Field, brothers who were fine hunters; Charles Floyd and Nathaniel Pryor, cousins who would become sergeants; and William Bratton and George Gibson, who would prove to be able salt makers during the expedition's winter on the Oregon coast. Clark had followed Lewis's directive, but he also knew when to bend a rule. John Shields, another of his candidates, was neither young nor unmarried, but he was a superb gunsmith whose skills would be invaluable as the men made their way through the wilderness.

When Lewis arrived at the Falls of Ohio in the fifty-five-foot keelboat he had brought down the Ohio River from Pittsburgh, these seven men were inducted into the army, along with George Shannon and John Colter, who had joined Lewis en route. Known today as the "nine young men from Kentucky," they formed the nucleus of the Corps of Discovery. Another man who joined the expedition at this point was York, a slave Clark had inherited from his father. The two had been boyhood companions, and York would travel with Clark to the Pacific and back as a member of the crew rather than as a personal servant.

Although the total number of men had already reached Jefferson's estimate of ten or twelve, recruitment would continue for months. Once Lewis learned of Napoleon Bonaparte's surprise decision to sell the Louisiana Territory to the United States, there was no further need for secrecy, as the expedition would no longer be passing through French-controlled land. The party traveling to the Northwest could now be much larger than originally planned.

A Diverse Group Becomes a Cohesive Team

About two weeks after leaving the Louisville area, the men reached Fort Massac, set on a promontory overlooking the Ohio River in

Bob Plummer, of Portland, Missouri, has portrayed George Drouillard, Jean Baptiste Deschamps, and other civilian crew members.

David Hibbler, of St. Charles, portrays Patrick Gass, who became a sergeant after the 1804 death of Sgt. Charles Floyd.

Peter Geery, of St. Charles, plays the role of Sgt. John Ordway, who kept his own thorough, day-by-day record of the expedition.

THE NEW CORPS OF DISCOVERY

The Missouri River town of St. Charles enjoys many special links to the Lewis and Clark expedition, and it is therefore appropriate that a St. Charles resident, the late Glen Bishop, created the perfect symbol for Missouri's chapter in that epic story. He spent twelve years handcrafting a full-scale replica of the fifty-five-foot keelboat used by the expedition. After the boat was destroyed in a 1997 warehouse fire, Glen became the guiding spirit for the Discovery Expedition of St. Charles, a nonprofit organization formed in 1997 to construct and crew full-size replicas of the keelboat and two pirogues used in the Missouri portion of the upriver voyage. The pirogues were completed in 1998, and the keelboat was finished in 2001, a few months before Glen died.

With 275 members, the Discovery Expedition strives to offer a living-history experience that is as authentic as possible. Most of the members are from Missouri, and about forty are from the St. Charles area. Like the men of the 1804-06 Corps of Discovery, these volunteers come from both civilian and military backgrounds and possess skills ranging from carpentry to cooking. New recruits must be trained in boat handling, certified in water safety, and knowledgeable about Lewis and Clark's era.

Members of the Discovery Expedition will retrace Meriwether Lewis's 1803 voyage down the Ohio River and the expedition's 1804-05 voyage up the Missouri River to Great Falls, Montana, as official reenactors in the national 2003-06 Lewis and Clark bicentennial commemoration. *Visit www.lewisandclark.net for more information and a schedule of reenactments.* —**Ann Rogers**

southern Illinois. Here, Lewis was able to hire the services of a civilian employee at the fort, George Drouillard, who would be one of the expedition's most valuable members. His father was a French Canadian, but Drouillard had been raised by his Shawnee mother in southeast Missouri, near Cape Girardeau. His abilities as a scout and his knowledge of American Indian languages, including sign language, caught the attention of Lewis, who knew the Corps of Discovery would be meeting with numerous tribes as the expedition moved through the Northwest.

According to plan, Lewis dismissed seven soldiers who had helped get the keelboat down the Ohio from Pittsburgh. He was unable, however, to find a number of soldiers at Fort Massac who were suitable and available for the long journey to the Pacific. He then asked Drouillard to travel about three hundred miles to South West Point, in Tennessee, and bring any recruits the commander there would release to meet the keelboat, which would be heading north on the Mississippi River.

Early in December 1803, Clark established a camp on the east bank of the Mississippi, about eighteen miles north of St. Louis, near the Wood River, then known as the River Dubois. While Lewis spent much of the winter in St. Louis, learning from fur merchants and mapmakers as much as he could about the lower Missouri River, Clark began training soldiers gathered from Fort Kaskaskia and other posts. On New Year's Day, Clark "put up a Dollar to be Shot for" in a marksmanship contest between his men and local residents. The "Countrey people" were the initial winners, but a winter of practice gave Clark's men the advantage in an April rematch.

Along with working to improve their skills, the men had to accept the discipline that military life imposes. Excessive drinking and fighting were not uncommon, and during the stay at Wood River, some men were dismissed as unsuitable, others chose to leave, and even the best could be unruly at times.

In the course of the journey, however, those who survived the selection process formed a cohesive unit and demonstrated individual abilities that benefited the corps. Silas Goodrich was a fine fisherman; Patrick Gass used his carpentry skills to build winter quarters; Joseph Whitehouse was adept at fashioning clothing from animal hides; and William Werner became an inventive cook when provisions were sparse. Even Joseph Collins, whose drinking was a problem in the first months, became one of the best hunters on the return trip.

Hard Work and Hunting Skills Sustain the Men
About ten days before the Corps of Discovery began its voyage up the Missouri River, seven French *engagés,* or hired boatmen, assembled by St. Louis fur merchant Auguste Chouteau, arrived at Camp Wood. Auguste Chouteau and his brother Pierre had assisted Lewis throughout the winter of preparation, and as the time for departure neared, they provided these experienced river men who knew the lower Missouri River. The *engagés* would form the crew of the red pirogue, one of two thirty-foot boats accompanying the keelboat.

Lewis and Clark selected Charles Floyd and Nathaniel Pryor to serve as sergeants along with John Ordway, an intelligent and responsible officer who already held that rank. These three were given rotating assignments that included steering the keelboat, managing the sails, making sure the oarsmen did their work, watching for obstructions in the river, and noting incoming rivers and streams. Assisting them on the keelboat were Pierre Cruzatte and François Labiche,

Discovery Expedition reenactors fire a salute to the state capitol.

who were recruited at St. Charles. Cruzatte was an able and experienced river man as well as a fiddler whose music would enliven celebrations and lift the crew's spirits during long winter encampments. Labiche, in addition to knowing the river, was fluent in both French and English, making him a valuable translator throughout the journey. Lewis assigned Labiche and Cruzatte to alternate manning the keelboat's larboard (left) bow oar as they watched for logs, snags, and other hazards near the shore.

Traveling northwest on the Missouri involved rowing against both the river's current and the prevailing winds. Days were long, and the midsummer heat was intense as the expedition moved through what is now western Missouri. Occasionally, a favorable breeze allowed the crew to raise the sail and take some rest from the oars, but at other times the men would have to jump into the water and struggle to pull the boat off sandbars with a towrope.

Feeding four dozen hardworking men called for skilled hunters who could shoot ample game, get it to the river, and accurately gauge how far the boats had traveled in their absence so that a rendezvous could be made. The expedition's youngest member, George Shannon, nearly died only weeks after the men left present-day Missouri, when he spent his bullets and then pushed on for sixteen days, desperately trying to catch up to the boats that were actually behind him. His misadventure began when he became separated from Drouillard, a far more experienced woodsman.

Although Drouillard had been hired as a scout and interpreter — services that would be vital later in the journey — in the first months, he was primarily a hunter. And he had no equal. It is his name, usu-

ally spelled "Drewyer," that appears most often when the expedition's journalists mention the successful hunters. He shot eight of the black bears killed during the 1804 crossing of Missouri, and on June 8, near today's town of Boonville, he killed five deer before noon.

The other leading hunters were the Field brothers and another of Clark's recruits, John Shields. Even before the Corps of Discovery reached the Northwest and faced mountainous terrain, bitter weather, and the threat of grizzlies, these men were tested. On June 2, just east of present-day Jefferson City, Clark wrote: "George Drewyer & John Shields who we had Sent with the horses by Land … joined us this evening much worsted, they being absent Seven Days. … the greater part of the time rain, they were obliged to raft or Swim many Creeks." Despite their ordeal, he reported that they "gave a flattering account of the Countrey."

"The Writingest Explorers of Their Time"

Clark called the hunters "our Spies," because they routinely brought back not only game to feed the party but also reports of what they had seen, including descriptions of woods and prairies that provided the expedition's journalists with an accurate picture of the landscape away from the river. President Jefferson had directed Lewis to learn as much as possible about the region to be traversed and to make multiple copies of the information as protection against accidental loss. Lewis, in turn, instructed each of his sergeants to "keep a seperate journal … of all passing occurences" and "observations of the country … as shall appear to them worthy of notice."

Other members of the party took up the practice, and during the crossing of Missouri, at least seven men were writing. Sergeant Charles Floyd's simple account, with his repeated praise for the Missouri landscape, was cut short when the young Kentuckian died on August 20, 1804. Patrick Gass, who became a sergeant after Floyd's death, kept a journal, as did Pvt. Joseph Whitehouse and Pvt. Robert Frazer. Years after the expedition ended, Frazer would read to Franklin County neighbors from his account, which has remained missing for nearly two centuries. By the time Sgt. John Ordway wrote "finis" on the last page of his journal on September 23, 1806, his remarkable chronicle contained an entry for every one of the 863 days of the journey. Despite the difficulties of the voyage, the Corps of Discovery's journalists made an extraordinary response to Jefferson's request for multiple records of the enterprise and became, in the words of one historian, "the writingest explorers of their time."

The journal keepers recorded the final crew changes at their winter camp in present-day North Dakota. On April 7, 1805, five members of the Corps of Discovery who had earlier manned the white pirogue, accompanied by several *engagés,* started back to St. Louis with the keelboat, which was considered too large for the upper Missouri. That same day a French interpreter named Touissant Charbonneau, his young Shoshone wife, Sacagawea, and their infant son joined the two captains and the remaining members of the Corps of Discovery as they continued westward, traveling in the two pirogues and six dugout canoes they made that spring.

Nineteen months and three thousand river miles after Lewis left Pittsburgh, the Lewis and Clark expedition was composed of the thirty-three persons who would go on to cross the Rockies and eventually reach the Pacific Ocean.

ABOUT THE AUTHOR: **Ann Rogers** is the author of *Lewis and Clark in Missouri.* A third edition of the book was published in 2002 by the University of Missouri Press.

From left: Each year, the Discovery Expedition of St. Charles reenacts part of Lewis and Clark's trek from Pennsylvania to Great Falls, Montana, beyond which the original keelboat and pirogues could not proceed. Their keelboat is fifty-five feet long and weighs seven tons.

HOME AT LONG LAST

By **Brett Dufur & Claire Griffis**

I N APRIL 1805, Lewis and Clark sent the keelboat and about a dozen men back downriver to St. Louis with maps, artifacts, and plant and animal specimens that they had collected up to this point. The rest of the party went on to the Pacific Ocean and then made the return trip to Missouri in a flotilla of dugout canoes hewn from huge cottonwood trees.

Late on a quiet Sunday afternoon, weary Corps of Discovery members dressed entirely in buckskin fired a three-gun salute as they eddied out of the main current of the Mighty Mo and nosed their canoes onto the muddy banks of St. Charles. Two days later, on September 23, 1806, they arrived to great fanfare at their final destination: St. Louis. The whole town turned out to welcome the returning explorers, who had been gone a total of two years and four months, traveling some eight thousand miles on their trip to the Pacific Ocean and back. "The party is considerably rejoiced that we have the expedition completed," Captain Lewis wrote.

Gone for more than two years, in part forgotten, even given up for dead, the Corps of Discovery's return cannot be summed up easily. Though the sheer fact that the men had survived might have been enough reason for celebration, for the captains, the return was surely a mixed bag. The expedition had, after all, failed in its ultimate mission: to find a navigable waterway to the Pacific Ocean. Even amid the celebratory atmosphere in St. Charles and St. Louis, this omission

MORE THAN TWO YEARS AFTER THE CORPS OF DISCOVERY BEGAN ITS ASCENT OF THE MISSOURI RIVER, THE EXPLORERS RETURNED TO THE STATE, AND SEVERAL OF THEM STAYED

From left: Lewis and Clark took detailed notes, made meticulous maps, and tried to illustrate the American Indians they encountered. Clark's famous journal was bound in elk skin.

was not forgotten by Lewis or Clark.

But due to the duration of the trip and the fact that only one man died along the way, one historian has called the odyssey "the most successful military expedition in U.S. history." And perhaps just as important to our fledgling nation as actually finding a waterway, Lewis and Clark have become icons for the seemingly unquenchable American desire to explore and to head west. They have become heroes, something that every country needs.

Having written more than 1.5 million words in their journals, the explorers were able to record an important moment in time for our country. They had encountered numerous American Indian tribes and had been able to record their way of life during an era when these cultures were largely unknown and untouched by the United States.

At the moment of the Corps of Discovery's return, the wilderness-hardened explorers must have experienced culture shock with their sudden fame and return to the accommodations of civilization. Just as their lives were now written into the legacy of the West, soon they would branch out and leave their impression on every aspect of life in the United States, becoming everything from farmers to politicians. Their time in the wilderness had helped to mold the strength, character, and confidence of the men, which is reflected in adventures that many of them would continue to seek out for the rest of their lives.

The artifacts shown are part of Lewis and Clark: The National Bicentennial Exhibition, *which will be on display at the Missouri History Museum at Forest Park at St. Louis from January 14 to September 6, 2004. The exhibit includes hundreds of artifacts and documents that have not been seen in one place since the Corps of Discovery returned to St. Louis in 1806. Call 314-746-4599, or visit www.mohistory.org for more information.*

After the expedition, the enlisted men were paid, given warrants for property west of the Mississippi, and discharged from service. Some crew members returned to their families and farms, while others returned to the frontier's allures, this time heading for the wealth and adventures to be found in the burgeoning beaver trade. But the roots of many of the men grew deeper during their time along the Missouri River, and many of them chose to make what would become the state of Missouri their home.

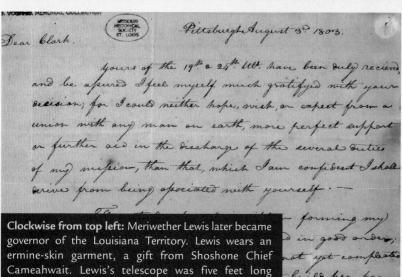

Pittsburgh, August 3rd 1803.

Dear Clark.

yours of the 19th & 24th Ult. have been duly recieved, and be assured I feel myself much gratifyed with your decision; for I could neither hope, wish, or expect from a union with any man on earth, more perfect support or further aid in the discharge of the several duties of my mission, than that, which I am confident I shall derive from being associated with yourself. —

Clockwise from top left: Meriwether Lewis later became governor of the Louisiana Territory. Lewis wears an ermine-skin garment, a gift from Shoshone Chief Cameahwait. Lewis's telescope was five feet long when extended. William Clark was officially made a captain in 2000. Lewis wrote to Clark in August 1803 to acknowledge Clark's decision to join the expedition.

The Captains

Lewis was committed to his shared leadership with Clark until the very end, even when government officials were preparing bonus rewards for expedition members. Since Lewis, a captain, was technically a higher ranking officer than Clark, a second lieutenant, Lewis was rewarded with sixteen hundred acres of land, while Clark was given only one thousand acres. True to his convictions, Lewis rebelled against this decision until the officials reconsidered the unequal compensation and decided to reward Clark with the same amount of land as Lewis had received.

Soon after their return, President Jefferson appointed Lewis the new governor of the Louisiana Territory. Far from the simpler days on the expedition, Lewis's duties now included unraveling incredibly complex political problems, including disputed French, Spanish, and American land titles. The bitter antagonism of the jealous territorial secretary, Frederick Bates, added to Lewis's problems. After two years as governor, several of Lewis's political drafts, as well as some he made during the expedition, were called into question by government clerks. In order to set things straight, settle expenses, and get the ball rolling on the publication of expedition journals, Lewis made his way to Washington, D.C., in the fall of 1809. Unfortunately, for a man already known for moods of melancholy, the problems and accusations he intended to clear up caused him great emotional strain. On October 11, 1809, while on the Natchez Trace, Lewis died at age thirty-five from either murder or suicide. A monument stands in his honor at his burial place near Hohenwald, Tennessee.

Early in 1807, Clark was made primary Indian agent for the Louisiana Territory and based his work out of St. Louis, on the grounds where the Gateway Arch is now located. Many American Indians would travel to St. Louis to share the grievances they had in varying disputes with white settlers. Clark was also appointed brigadier general of the Louisiana militia, and he remained in both of these positions for the rest of his life. After the return of the expedition, Clark called for "Pompey," Sacagawea's young son, whose true name was Jean Baptiste, to be brought to Clark's home in St. Louis, where Clark acted as Pompey's guardian and raised him as his own child. Clark married his childhood sweetheart, Julie Hancock, from Fincastle, Virginia, and the happy newlyweds took their honeymoon on the Ohio River in January 1808. Julia and William Clark had four sons, the first of whom they named Meriwether Lewis Clark, and one daughter. In June 1813, Clark was appointed governor of the Louisiana Territory after his friend and partner Lewis died, and he held the position until 1820. On June 27, 1820, Julia died of an undocumented illness at age twenty-eight.

Clark later married Julia's cousin, Harriet Kennerly, a widow. They had two sons, but only one lived past childhood. On September 1, 1838, at the age of sixty-eight, Clark died in St. Louis. He is buried at Bellefontaine Cemetery at St. Louis, where a monument at his grave reads, "Soldier, Explorer, Statesman and Patriot, His Life Is Written In the History of His Country." In November 2000, more than 150 years after his death, Clark was finally given the official title of co-captain of the Corps of Discovery expedition.

The Crew

York, Clark's slave, was finally freed by Clark in 1811, and he later married in Kentucky. Clark gave him six horses and a dray, or cart, which York used to start a wagon freight company. The freight business transported items between Nashville, Tennessee, and Richmond, Kentucky, but had failed by 1832. York started drinking heavily, telling adventure stories from the expedition all the while. As the stories got bigger and bigger, York got closer and closer to death. On his way to visit Clark, York died of cholera in Tennessee by 1832.

On August 13, 1806, while on his way home, Pvt. John Colter was discharged from the army with honors. With trappers Forrest Hancock and Joseph Dickson, he went back west to the Yellowstone River, where he remained for about six months. After half a year together, there was a falling out between the men, and Colter headed back to St. Louis. He entered Manuel Lisa's trapping party, and with them, he started back for Yellowstone. Colter arrived by October 1807, trapped for several years, and then returned to St. Louis by 1809.

While there, Colter sold his land warrant and joined another trapping party that was headed up the Missouri River into Blackfoot Indian territory. Colter had been friends with the Crows, the enemy of the Blackfeet, and during his six years of trapping in the area, he is said to have scalped nearly a hundred Blackfeet. As the story goes, after meeting up with John Potts at the Three Forks of the Missouri River, the two encountered eight hundred Blackfeet. Potts, who did not want to be taken prisoner, was killed. Afterward, Colter was taken prisoner and stripped of his clothes. After Colter claimed he was a bad runner, the Indians told him to run for his life. The Blackfeet then pursued him after giving him a few hundred yards as a head start. Colter, who was actually an excellent and adept hunter, ran with so much speed that he quickly separated himself from the angry Blackfeet.

As some of the pack gained on him, Colter ran harder, dripping blood from injuries in his nose and mouth and from sheer effort. With only a mile between himself and the river, Colter faced a spear-bearing Indian. He wrestled the Indian to the ground with the Indian's own weapon before taking it and a blanket and then running for safety again. Colter hid in beaver dens when he could. He traveled constantly with little rest, stopping for meals of tree bark and roots. Eleven days after the attack, Colter arrived at Manuel Lisa's nearby fort with misshapen, swollen feet.

During his escape, Colter became the first white man to witness Yellowstone's geyser eruptions, a phenomenon many people believed to be a lie. After his ordeal, the Yellowstone area became known as Colter's Hell. In 1810, Colter married an Indian woman known as Sallie and the two moved to a farm close to present-day Franklin County, Missouri. Colter and Sallie had one son, named Hiram. Colter died on November 22, 1813, and was buried near his home, at Dundee, Missouri, on Tunnel Hill. During his life, Colter designed a map of the Northwest, which he gave to William Clark. He also tried unsuccessfully to collect $377.60 from Lewis's estate on May 28, 1811, probably for extra pay for his time with the Corps

THE LEWIS AND CLARK EXPEDITION WAS THE GREATEST ADVENTURE OF THE CREW MEMBERS' LIVES.

of Discovery, but the estate was bankrupt. In December 1814 Colter's possessions went up for auction and raised only $124.44. This money went to Sallie, who later remarried and died after 1822.

After the expedition's return, Interpreter George Drouillard settled in Cape Girardeau. He bought the land warrants of expedition members John Collins and Joseph Whitehouse, and by selling them and other properties, Drouillard earned thirteen hundred dollars. He soon made a trip back to the Rocky Mountains and took detailed topographical notes, which he gave to Clark. Clark used these notes to make his map of the Northwest. In 1810, while with Manuel Lisa's party, Drouillard was killed by the Blackfoot Indians at the Three Forks of the Missouri River.

Sgt. John Ordway bought the land warrants of expedition members William Werner and Jean Baptiste La Page. Afterward, Ordway accompanied Lewis and a party of Indians to visit Washington, D.C. He settled in the Tywappity Bottom area, near New Madrid, Missouri, in 1809. He married a woman named Gracy, and he died in 1817.

In 1809, Lewis loaned money to Pvt. Hugh Hall, who was reported to be in St. Louis. He was said to still be living in 1828.

In 1808, Pvt. Thomas Proctor Howard was serving in the army.

He married Genevieve Roy in St. Louis and had a son, Joseph.

After the expedition, Pvt. Hugh McNeal stayed in the army until September 1811. Clark listed him as dead by the late 1820s.

On July 5, 1832, Pvt. John Newman married Olympia Dubreuil, of St. Louis. From 1834 to 1838, Newman traded on the upper Missouri River. He was killed in 1838 by Yankton Sioux Indians.

Pvt. John Boley was part of the party that returned to St. Louis in 1805, led by Cpl. Richard Warfington. That same year, he joined Zebulon Pike's party to search for the sources of the Mississippi River. Boley also went with Pike to the Rocky Mountains. He arrived in New Orleans in February 1807 with a party that went down the Arkansas River. After his parents died, Boley inherited their home and property in Missouri. Some people believe that Boley was part of a later expedition to the mountains. Boley and his wife were living in Carondelet, Missouri, in October 1823.

In August 1804, Pvt. Moses Reed was expelled from the party for attempting to desert. He was sentenced to hard labor, and he remained with the expedition until he was sent back to St. Louis with the return party in 1805. In 1807, Reed received $180 in back pay and $178.50 in bonus pay. Like the other men, he was given a land warrant, which was for property in Franklin County, Missouri.

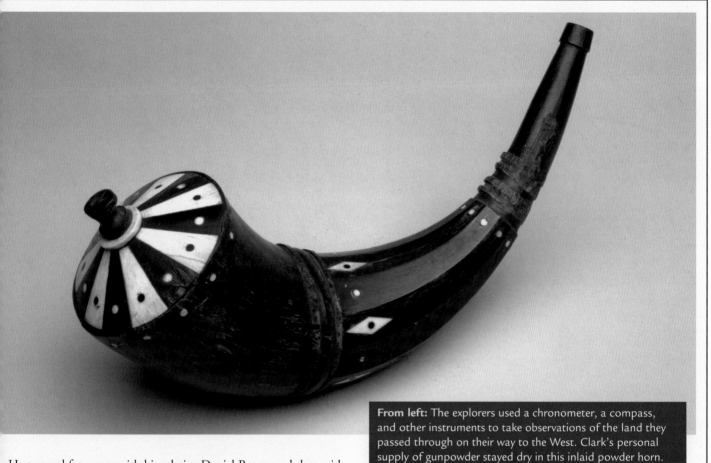

He trapped for a year with his relative Daniel Boone and then with Squire Boone in Indiana. He died in December 1809 and was survived by his wife, Nancy, and daughter, Janette.

On March 11, 1807, Lewis sent Pvt. William Werner $30.75, a horse, saddle, and other items valued at $44.50. Under the conditions of this arrangement, Clark was instructed to deduct the price of the horse from Werner's pay if the animal died of negligence or if Werner sold the horse. For a while after the expedition's return, Werner assisted Clark as an Indian agent in Missouri. By 1828, Werner was reported to be alive in Virginia.

Pvt. Joseph Whitehouse sold his bonus land warrant of 160 acres to George Drouillard for $280. In 1807, he was arrested in St. Louis for debt, but he was free by 1812, when he joined the army to serve in the war. Five years later, Whitehouse deserted his station, and his whereabouts were later unknown.

In 1807, as a member of a party led by Sgt. Nathaniel Pryor and charged with escorting the Mandan Chief Sheheke to his home in what is now North Dakota, Pvt. George Shannon lost one of his legs in an encounter with the Arikara Indians. He later practiced law in Kentucky and then became active in Missouri politics. Shannon died in 1836 and was buried at Palmyra, Missouri.

Pvt. George Gibson entertained the men by playing the fiddle during the expedition. He may have been with the party that escorted Chief Sheheke in 1807, and he also may have been wounded during that trip. He died in St. Louis in 1809.

Pvt. Robert Frazier went to Washington, D.C., and Virginia with Lewis but returned to St. Louis and was given a land warrant on October 6, 1806. He was in the militia serving against the Aaron Burr plotters in St. Louis and New Orleans. He had found evidence of treason and was a witness at the trial. Frazier had a few run-ins with the law, and from 1825, he lived near the Gasconade River in Missouri. He died in Franklin County in 1837. During his life, Frazier drew maps of the Northwest that he intended to publish with his journal from the expedition. These maps are now in the Library of Congress.

The historical record is not clear, but an *engagé*, or boatman, named La Liberté may be the man known as Joseph La Liberte who married Julie Village on January 11, 1835, in St. Louis and was buried in there on May 31, 1837.

Pvt. François (William) Labiche went with Lewis to Washington, D.C., acting as an interpreter for the group of Indians they were accompanying. Labiche may be the same man known as François Labuche, who married a Genevieve Flore and baptized seven children between 1811 and 1834. Labiche was reported to be alive in St. Louis after 1828.

Toussaint Charbonneau worked under Manuel Lisa and Clark as an interpreter while Clark was the head of Indian Affairs. He died in 1866 and is buried at Richwoods, Missouri, where he is said to have owned a mining company and operated a trading post.

Pvt. John Shields joined his relative Daniel Boone to trap furs in Missouri. Afterward, he settled in Indiana and then died in 1809.

Certainly, the Lewis and Clark expedition had been the greatest adventure many of these men would see in their lives. The crew of the Corps of Discovery wove seamlessly into many diverse aspects of that new material — that new West — that would forever change the American flag. Today, many descendants of Lewis, Clark, and their crew members live in Missouri and keep the adventurous spirit of the Corps of Discovery alive.

"BUTIFULL COUNTREY"

By Kathy Love

THE JOURNALS OF the Corps of Discovery are full of observations about the new territory that eventually came to be called Missouri. The explorers described a "butifull countrey … interspursed with Praries & timber alturnetly." They wrote of land "covered with lofty and excellent timber" and "a place of great resort for Deer and fowls of every kind."

The expedition's route through Missouri teemed with fish and wildlife that fed the hungry men. William Clark estimated that the crew needed four deer, or an elk and a deer, or one buffalo per day to fuel the journey west. Missouri abounded in these animals, and the river route was also rich with edible plants and fish.

Two hundred years later, there have been massive changes to the Missouri River and its surrounding countryside. Some fish and wildlife populations were decimated, never to return. Others are here in abundance, once again, after conservation efforts helped restore their populations. Prairies have been plowed until only a fragment of that native ecosystem remains. The same is true for wetlands, which were diked, dammed, and drained, resulting in the loss of systems that once naturally slowed and filtered floodwater. Forests along the river were cut to feed the boilers of steamboats. But travelers along the route of Lewis and Clark can still see plants, animals, and ecosystems that make Missouri "a butifull countrey."

"… affection in every bud that opens"

"There is not a sprig of grass that shoots uninteresting to me," wrote Thomas Jefferson, who also said he had "an interest or affection in every bud that opens, in every breath that blows around me." His ability as a naturalist was well known and an early influence on his young secretary, Meriwether Lewis, whom Jefferson would send to explore the then-unknown lands of the American West.

Lewis meticulously documented more than 239 species of plants unknown to botanists at the time. His writing and the journals of his crew reveal that the Missouri River valley was a cornucopia of native plants that were both useful and beautiful.

Edible wild plants supplemented the Corps of Discovery's protein-rich meat diet with much-needed vitamins and minerals. "Strawbury in the prairies ripe and abundant," Sergeant John Ordway wrote in May 1804, of the area near the settlement of La Charrette. Two days later he observed, "Servisburries or wild Courants, ripe and abundant." On June 5, Clark noted that "York swam to [an island] to pick greens" for dinner. He returned with "a Sufficient quantity [of] wild [Cresses] or Teng [Tongue] grass."

IN MISSOURI, THE CORPS OF DISCOVERY FOUND LUSH PLANTS, ABUNDANT GAME, AND HUGE CATFISH

They also found berries, grapes, nuts, and "plumbs." On June 10, Clark wrote "I discovered a Plumb which grows on bushes the hight of Hasle, those plumbs are … double the Sise of the wild plumb."

River travelers today would have a hard time living on the wild fruit of the land. The once-braided flow of the Missouri River has been tamed into a single, deep channel by levees and dikes. The land that accreted behind the dikes has been cultivated with rows of crops that provide food of a more marketable sort. However, plums, berries, and nuts can still be found along bluffs and in the margins between the river and levees.

Competition from exotic plants has also crowded out native plants. Johnson grass, purple loosestrife, and garlic mustard are introduced, invasive species that colonize vulnerable sites like flood plains. Native wild plants such as Alpine rush, knotted rush, and bushy cinquefoil, once abundant on the sandy ground and mudflats of the Missouri River, have not been found there for more than fifty years.

"Caught two verry fat Cat fish"

When Lewis and Clark traveled up the Mississippi River to St. Louis, they remarked on the abundance of large catfish in the river. Lewis was "a little surprised at the apparent size of a Catfish which the men had caught … although we had been previously accustomed to see those of from thirty to sixty pounds weight." They lacked a scale large

Above: The men killed at least a dozen bears before reaching the Kansas River. **Left:** On June 20, 1804, Clark noted seeing pelicans on a sandbar. They were likely American white pelicans.

The papaw, also called the Missouri banana, grows along the river and ripens in early fall.

GOBBLING SNAKES AND NIGHTINGALES

The Corps of Discovery contributed significantly to scientific knowledge of the plants and animals west of the Mississippi, but they also confounded scientists and others with fantastic tales of animal encounters.

One of the most puzzling is the gobbling snake. On June 14, as the party camped near what is now Van Meter State Park, at Miami, Missouri, Clark wrote, "G. Drewyer tels of a remarkable Snake inhabiting a Small lake 5 ms. below which gobbles like a Turkey & may be herd Several miles. ..." In another entry from this day, he adds "he fired his gun & the noise was increased, he has heard the indians Mention This Species of Snake one Frenchman give a Similar account."

Historians and naturalists attribute the story to overactive imaginations or a practical joke. More puzzling, though, is Clark's reference to a nightingale on June 4, 1804, in the area that is now Jefferson City. He names a creek "Nightingale" for "a Bird of that description which Sang for us all last night, and is the first of the Kind I ever heard."

There are no true nightingales in the United States, so there are many theories about the bird whose song they heard. Speculation ranges from the Chuck-wills-widow to the wood thrush to the yellow-breasted chat. The creek long ago lost its "nightingale" name. Now it's known as the Moreau River.

THE PAPAW PUZZLE

On their return through Missouri in September 1806, Lewis, Clark, and their men sped down the river, sometimes making seventy-five miles in one day. As they neared their destination, rather than take time to hunt for game, as they did on their way up the river two years before, they relied on papaws — a fruit abundant along the banks of the Missouri River — for a major portion of their diet.

On September 15, 1806, Clark wrote, "we landed one time only to let the men geather Pappaws or the Custard apple of which this Country abounds, and the men are very fond of." On September 18, two days before they arrived at La Charrette, Clark wrote, "...our party entirely out of provisions Subsisting on poppaws ... the party appear perfectly contented and tell us that they can live very well on the pappaws."

At the same time, many of the men experienced a mysterious condition in which their eyes became swollen and irritated. Clark wrote on September 19, "a very singular disorder is taking place amongst our party that of the Sore eyes. three of the party have their eyes inflamed and Sweled in Such a manner as to render them extreamly painfull. ..."

Botanical references often cite papaws as the source of a "minor and temporary skin irritation or a painful irritation and inflammation." Ann Rogers, author of *Lewis and Clark in Missouri*, believes it is likely that papaws were the source of the irritation.

"It was a hot September, and they were exerting themselves to get home," Ann says. "I can imagine them handling papaws one minute and wiping sweat from their eyes the next. Of course, we'll never know for sure." —Kathy Love

enough to weigh the fish so they weighed it in sections, estimating its total weight by this method at 128 pounds.

On July 4, 1804, at a lake near present-day Kansas City, the men also noted an "abundance of fish of various species, the pike, catt, sunfish & ... perch carp, or buffaloe fish." On July 17, in northwest Missouri, Clark wrote that Silas Goodrich "caught two verry fat Cat Fish." On July 29, Clark wrote, "those Cat [fish] are So plenty that they may be Cought in any part of this river."

The 1900s brought changes that were meant to speed cargo barges up and down the river by creating a deep channel without obstacles or shallow areas, but these changes also drastically altered conditions for fish. Fish like sturgeon require shallow areas on which to spawn, and catfish use snags and cavities along the riverbank.

In the 1960s, a fortunate accident led the way to better habitat. A fisheries biologist noticed that some of the wing dikes that force the river into its narrow channel were in need of repair. Water plunged through gaps in the broken dikes, creating deep holes on the downstream side and shallow habitat upstream. Rather than repairing the gaps, engineers agreed to modify other dikes to expand habitat.

Commercial catfishing was closed in 1994 to stem the tide of over-harvest, but it was the floods of 1993 and 1995 that were most beneficial to fish populations. Flood conditions limited the catch and created an abundance of food and new habitat for fish. Now, catfish are rebounding, but others, like the endangered pallid sturgeon, still suffer from lack of habitat.

"... emence numbs. of Deer on the banks, Skipping in every derection"

A close look at the journals of Lewis and Clark reveals that deer were observed and hunted almost daily in Missouri. They killed their first deer May 19, 1804, in St. Charles. Seven were killed near present-day Jefferson City on June 4. On June 8, George Drouillard killed five before noon. Eight deer were killed June 24, five on June 28, and nine on June 30, when Clark noted "emence numbs. of Deer on the banks, Skipping in every derection."

On June 6 and 7, the Corps trailed some buffalo without success. Clark wrote on June 7, "Som Buffalow Sign Sent out George Drewyer & Newmon to hunt. ..." On June 28, the hunters saw buffalo on the Kansas River, but it was not until they entered Nebraska that Lewis saw one. The men shot their first buffalo August 23, 1804.

Although Clark wrote on June 17 that the country "abounds" in elk, they proved elusive. The first were sighted in what is now Nebraska, when Lewis's dog, Seaman, chased them into the river.

Bears made up a big portion of the crew's diet. On June 7, Clark

From Top: Near the site of Kansas City, Lewis and Clark saw Carolina parakeets and had their first encounters with beavers.

wrote, "our hunters brought in 3 bear this evening." Whitehouse describes them as "One Old famel & her two Cubbs brought in by G. Drewyer." On June 15, Floyd wrote, "Good Level Land ouer hunters killed 4 Bars and 3 Deer."

The men dried extra meat for future use. On June 11, Clark wrote, "Drewyer Killed two Bear in the Prarie. ... we had the meat Jurked and also the Venison, which is a Constant Practice to have all the fresh meat not used, Dried in this way."

The Corps encountered predators, too. On June 28, Ordway wrote, "R. & J. Fields killed a young woolf & brought one home to camp for to Tame." The latter was kept for three days and then escaped. Two days later Clark wrote, "a verry large wolf Came to the bank and looked at us this morning."

The men called coyotes "little prarie wolves" and noted their resemblance to domesticated dogs. Lewis described the eastern wood rat, a species new to science, at Ft. Clatsop, Oregon, but their first sighting occurred in Missouri on May 31, 1804. Clark wrote, "Several rats of Considerable Size was Cought in the woods to day." Patrick Gass summed up the species with a single observation: "The principal difference between it and the common rat is, its having hair on its tail."

In June 1804, the explorers saw flocks of a bright green, yellow, and red bird, the Carolina parakeet. The explorers were the first to record sightings of the birds west of the Mississippi. The birds' colorful plumage became their downfall when feathered hats became fashionable, luring hunters to shoot them by the hundreds. The Carolina parakeet became extinct in 1913.

Wildlife sustained, intrigued, and amazed the Corps of Discovery. Some of the species they described that were incompatible with early settlers, such as the wolf, bear, bison, and elk (the latter two because of their need for large grazing areas), were eliminated. The grass-roots conservation movement of the last century, however, brought back native fish, forests, and wildlife to Missouri. George Drouillard would be pleased today to learn deer, wild turkey, and waterfowl are once again plentiful in this "butifull countrey."

ABOUT THE AUTHOR AND ILLUSTRATIONS: Kathy Love is a writer and editor for the Missouri Department of Conservation. Journal excerpts were compiled by Ann Rogers, author of *Lewis and Clark in Missouri*. Several of the illustrations shown come from the exhibit "Objects Worthy of Notice," which combines the art of John James Audubon with information about species described by Lewis and Clark. It was put together by the State Historical Society of Missouri and the U.S. Fish and Wildlife Service and designed by the Department of Conservation.

CORPS OF CREATIVITY

By Sadie Grabill, Jo Beck, and Sona Pai

Paul Jackson's Watercolor Explorations

Paul Jackson saw an opportunity in the bicentennial anniversary of Lewis and Clark's journey of discovery. It was the perfect chance to do what he says the greatest artists in history have done — create a visual interpretation of the past.

So Paul, a nationally recognized watercolor artist who lives in Columbia, began reading every one of Lewis and Clark's journal entries along with several books on the Corps of Discovery. Those readings sparked his imagination, and with a little extra historical research, he began to paint his interpretation of the journey in stunning watercolors.

In the dozen Lewis and Clark paintings Paul has created so far, he has focused on their time in Missouri because of his own interest in Missouri's waterways. Also, on the return trip, the expedition traveled through Missouri on a flotilla of canoes, and since Missouri means "people of big canoes," Paul thought it would be fitting to show Lewis and Clark paddling across the state's major waterway, the Missouri River.

Though his artistic mind created these first paintings, Paul decided to turn to the landscape of the explorers' journey for more inspiration. In August 2003, he and his brother Peter, who is a photographer, followed Lewis and Clark's trail and eventually traveled on to Alaska via the "asphalt passage," as Paul calls the highways that took them there. It was a twelve-thousand-mile round trip, and Paul spent much of it painting and sketching along the way. He saw some of the landscapes and vistas that Lewis and Clark saw two hundred

MISSOURI ARTISTS DEPICT THE LORE, LANDSCAPES, AND LEGACY OF LEWIS AND CLARK

years ago, and the six-week trip gave him fuel for future paintings.

Paul feels the legacy of Lewis and Clark is so important to Missouri that he depicted the explorers on a design that was selected for Missouri's commemorative state quarter. The design shows two men in a canoe on the Missouri River, and Paul says it is meant to remind people of Lewis and Clark.

"I wanted it to show the spirit of exploration," he says. "Missouri was the start of many great explorations."

And the Corps of Discovery's journey, perhaps the most significant of those explorations, will forever be memorialized not only on Missouri's quarter but also on Paul's canvases.

Call 573-875-2846 for more information, or visit www.pauljackson.com.
—*Sadie Grabill*

From left: Columbia artist Paul Jackson researched the Corps of Discovery expedition and painted *Council Fires* and *Lewis and Clark.*

Gary Lucy's Paintings of the Past

Rivers are a defining part of Gary Lucy's life. He lives on the Missouri River in Washington, Missouri, and he frequently follows some of the nation's major rivers on floating excursions. Rivers are also the subjects of an art exhibit Gary has been working on for several years, titled *Inland Waterways, the Highways of Our Heritage.*

The exhibit will be shown at the Old Courthouse in downtown St. Louis for five months beginning in September 2004. At its center will be Gary's oil paintings of Lewis and Clark on the rivers that carried the Corps of Discovery on its legendary journey.

Gary began his painting career as a wildlife artist, but after Lyle Woodcock — who advised Thomas Hart Benton during his career — suggested that Gary try painting the human figure, Gary combined his interests in water, history, and the people of the river to begin telling the story of the state's river heritage.

"Historical interpretation is one of the most valuable things an artist can do," Gary says. "The artist puts on canvas what's in his head. He can read about something, conjure an image in his head, and take those feelings and emotions and transfer them to canvas."

Gary did much reading and imagining about Lewis and Clark before painting them, but he also took pains to ensure the historical accuracy of his images. He commissioned a model-builder to create miniature versions of the boats the Corps of Discovery traveled in, and he used these models as references for his paintings. He also had experts replicate the explorers' uniforms — right down to the correct number of buttons — before he painted them.

Gary gets most of his inspiration not from books and his imagination, however, but from following the paths of Lewis and Clark

From left: Wildwood artist Michael Haynes climbed Tavern Rock to paint *Meriwether Lewis Escapes Death above Tavern Cave.* Washington artist Gary Lucy's Lewis and Clark series includes *Campsite at Tavern Creek, May 23, 1804,* and *The Departure from St. Charles, May 21, 1804.*

himself — on rivers, of course. Gary has followed Corps of Discovery reenactors for weeks at a time on various journeys. In 1998 he traveled with them from Yankton, South Dakota, to St. Charles, on the Missouri River, and in 1999 he traveled the Ohio River. In 2003 he spent five weeks on the Ohio River following reenactors. He follows them in his "river studio," a boat that is both a home and a place to work. This gives him an opportunity to study the characters from a distance, and he paints and sketches as he goes.

Gary says it's important to document Lewis and Clark's journey because their travels represent the country's first link between the Atlantic and Pacific Oceans. He also says the story of the pair's time in Missouri has escaped visual interpretation, so he has taken the task upon himself in a series of paintings called *Lewis and Clark: The Journey Begins,* which details the first seventy miles of their trip.

Gary has created nine Lewis and Clark paintings, and his images range from the Corps of Discovery at port, preparing for the journey, to peaceful scenes of the expedition floating amid Missouri's wilderness.

Visit www.garylucy.com, or call 800-937-4944 for more information. *—Sadie Grabill*

Michael Haynes's Realistic Re-creations

Michael Haynes creates paintings so lifelike you could fall in, and if you did, you'd find yourself in the 1800s. Michael, a Wildwood resident, has forged a national reputation as an artist of the Civil War and Lewis and Clark eras.

A self-described perfectionist, Michael researches historical figures until he gets the details as accurate as possible. In the case of one Lewis and Clark painting, getting the details right meant a pre-dawn trip to a cave in Franklin County, near St. Albans, for the painting *Meriwether Lewis Escapes Death above Tavern Cave.*

> "HISTORICAL INTERPRETATION IS ONE OF THE MOST VALUABLE THINGS AN ARTIST CAN DO."
>
> *—GARY LUCY*

"This near-tragedy happened when the expedition was only on its second day out from St. Charles, on May 23, 1804," Michael says. "Early that morning the expedition stopped about one mile above the Femme Osage River. There, they explored Tavern Cave, a popular Missouri River spot frequented by Indians and trappers. Pinnacles of rock towered three hundred feet above the water at this point."

While William Clark was adding his name to the register on the cave wall, Lewis decided to climb to the top of the bluff for a better look around. While near the top of the precipice, Lewis lost his foothold and slid twenty feet down the rock face. Just short of disaster, he "saved himself by the assistance of his Knife," Clark would write later in his journal.

"On the anniversary of this event, I climbed the bluffs to set the scene for the painting," Michael says. "Up on the bluffs I was struck by the composure and presence of mind that Lewis must have had to stop his fall by jamming his knife into the bluff. Jefferson's choice of Lewis as leader of this pivotal mission was reaffirmed to me on that spot."

Michael recently completed a series of five Lewis and Clark paintings commissioned by the U.S. Army Corps of Engineers. Those paintings are currently touring the country, and he is speaking about the paintings at various locations along the trail.

Michael's artwork has been featured in signs, films, brochures, and other literature to promote the Corps of Discovery's bicentennial and can be found all along the Lewis and Clark route. The U.S. Postal service is using his paintings of York and Sacagawea for a special-edition commemorative booklet. Currently, Michael is planning *Drawn Through Time,* a nationally touring exhibition of his prints accompanied by descriptive panels.

Michael's collaboration with historian Robert Moore to research and illustrate the uniforms of the expedition led to what has quickly become a Bible for interpreters, reenactors, and Lewis and Clark historians. Titled *Tailor Made, Trail Worn,* this coffee-table book published by FarCountry Press is lavishly illustrated with more than a hundred of Michael's paintings and drawings.

The state of Missouri has commissioned some of Michael's paintings for a 2004 wayside signage project that will promote and commemorate the Lewis and Clark expedition.

Call 636-458-0802, or visit www.mhaynesart.com for more information. —*Jo Beck*

Stuart Morse's Artful Expeditions

In 2000, St. Louis artist Stuart Morse, his wife Stacey, and his two young children, daughter Merill and son True, began a three-year quest to travel the Lewis and Clark trail. Stacey can trace her family lineage back to both Lewis and Clark, and the couple has always been interested in the explorers and their historic expedition. The first year, Stuart and family traveled from their home to Kansas.

Then, in 2001, they traveled to Pierre, South Dakota. And in 2002, they traveled all the way to the Pacific Ocean.

"We used a laptop computer and topographical GPS software to determine the highest points we could reach along the trail in each state," Stuart says. "Then we traveled on dirt and gravel roads up to those points in a vehicle rigged with a platform on top to hold a camera. All in all we took about nine thousand pictures of the route."

Stuart also sketched the landscapes he saw along the way. When he returned to his studio, he began a monumental project to document the unique landscapes of each state he visited on five-by-eleven-foot canvases. "I felt that, in terms of the art that was being created about Lewis and Clark, so much energy was going into depicting scenes from two hundred years ago," he says. "I wanted to show how the river sits within the modern landscape two centuries after Lewis and Clark passed through."

Stuart's paintings depict points along the trail that he feels best illustrate each state's character today. Each is dominated by natural

features but also includes indications of modern life, such as cultivated land, buildings, and signs of industry.

"There's something so pristine about seeing a little farm dwarfed by a roaring river that still hasn't really been tamed," Stuart says. "It shows that the river and the communities that have grown up around it are still worthy of exploration today."

Each of Stuart's ten massive landscapes is designed to be a flagship painting that will be exhibited in its respective state. The series is being recreated in limited edition prints, and a special set of prints will be part of a traveling exhibit that will stop at locations along the Lewis and Clark route. Stuart's Missouri painting, *A Journey's Quiet Guide,* is currently hanging at the state capitol at Jefferson City, where it will be on display through 2006. The painting features a view of the Missouri River, looking west from St. Albans, and it includes the hardwood forest stands, rocky bluffs, farmland, narrow river channel, and wing dikes that Stuart feels set the Missouri scenery apart from what he saw in other states.

"Of course the bicentennial is about looking back at the past," Stuart says. "But it should also be about exploring the people in today's communities and the landscapes they live in. These people and places are important parts of the legacy of Lewis and Clark."

Call 636-458-0886, or visit www.morsefineart.com for more information. —*Sona Pai*

Clockwise from left: Michael Haynes's *Moreau River* is part of a series of Lewis and Clark paintings. *A Swim with Jim and Nancy* is one of several paintings by St. Louis artist Stuart Morse that features the river landscape. His painting, *A Journey's Quiet Guide,* shows a spot on the Lewis and Clark trail near St. Albans, Missouri.

TOURING THE GREAT MISSOURI RIVER

By **Brett Dufur**

A S THE BICENTENNIAL commemoration of Lewis and Clark's 1804-06 voyage gets underway, it's ironic that modern-day explorers spend little time on the Missouri River, especially here, in the state where the Corps of Discovery, for all practical purposes, began and ended its trip. The Missouri River has developed the Grand Canyon Syndrome. That is, people drive up to see it, get out of their air-conditioned cars, and photograph it. Perhaps they walk along its banks for a bit, but then they get back in their cars and move on to the next spot. Although many Missourians have enjoyed spectacular views of the Missouri River, it seems as though few people realize the host of opportunities available to enjoy and to reconnect with the Missouri River valley.

Now that the Lewis and Clark expedition is fresh in our minds, it's time for Missourians to explore the river that served as the Corps of Discovery's superhighway to the West. The Missouri River was the site of some of Lewis and Clark's greatest adventures and most serene moments. It was their training ground for the unknown lands that lay ahead and their gateway to Missouri's verdant beauty and lush flora and fauna.

As Henry David Thoreau once said, "In Wildness is the preservation of the World." And so, it only seems appropriate that in this time of global uncertainty, nature should regain its prominent place

PLAN YOUR OWN EXPEDITION BY BARGE, BOAT, BIKE, BUS, OR EVEN BY HOT-AIR BALLOON

in our psyche. Today, you can see the river from the exact or at least similar vantage points as Lewis and Clark did and enjoy a front-row seat to the Lewis and Clark trail that cannot be found anywhere else.

Whether you are looking for a comfortable seat aboard a river barge, a tour aboard a small motorboat, the ease of a bus, or the breeze to be found on a bike or in a canoe, there have never been more ways to enjoy the Missouri River, the beautiful scenery around it, and the communities situated along its course through Missouri.

By Boat

A relatively new option for exploring the Missouri River is available from RiverBarge Excursion Lines, Inc. RiverBarge offers the most stately option for experiencing the Big Muddy without getting your toes wet. Ride aboard the 198-guest, 730-foot long *R/B River Explorer,* the only hotel barge traveling America's inland waterways. Offering a complete vacation package, "Barging Through America" allows guests to experience the river while also providing ample opportunities to visit river towns along the way. The fifty-foot tall, multistory barge is actually comprised of two barges, each 295 feet long, which are propelled by a three-thousand-horsepower towboat.

Onboard historians, entertainers from around the region, homestyle dining, and comfortable amenities make this a popular option

Left: Viewed from the deck of a barge, the setting sun provides a luminous backdrop for the serene Missouri River. **Right:** Boaters with their own small craft can tour the river more quickly and more comfortably than Lewis and Clark did.

Cruising along in a river barge is a scenic and relaxing way to explore the Missouri River today.

The Katy Trail follows Lewis and
Clark's trail along the Missouri River
from St. Charles to Boonville.

Bikers on the Katy Trail can follow alongside Lewis and Clark's river path.

for exploring the Missouri River valley. Tours ply the river between St. Louis and Kansas City. A nine-day excursion from St. Charles to Kansas City, called the Voyage of Discovery, is scheduled for 2004. Visit www.riverbarge.com, or call 888-GO-BARGE for more information. See "Rolling on the River," in the June 2001 issue of *Missouri Life* to learn more.

Big River Tours, based at Lexington, offers half-day and all-day small boat tours for up to six people on the Missouri River in central and western Missouri. Tours include Picnic Cruises, Kansas City Cruises, Big Muddy National Fish and Wildlife Refuge Cruises, Fort Osage Day Trips, Evening Cruises, and private charter opportunities. Prices range from twenty-five dollars per person for hour-long tours to eight hundred dollars per person for day-long excursions. For more information, call 816-470-3206, or visit www.bigrivertours.com.

If you'd like to tour the Missouri River in your own boat, be sure to familiarize yourself with standard navigation and safety procedures. For more information on boating on the river and maps that show boat ramps and fueling facilities, call 866-285-3219 to order the free *Lewis & Clark Bicentennial Lower Missouri River Guide to Recreation and Visitors Safety* from the U.S. Army Corps of Engineers.

Missouri Life's special publication, the *Lewis and Clark Discovery Guide,* includes the same maps along with Lewis and Clark events and festivals around the state. For more information about the guide, call 800-492-2593, ext. 101.

By Bike

Missourians who want to travel along the Lewis and Clark trail without hitting the water can follow the explorers' footsteps along the Katy Trail State Park. Stretching across the state for more than 225 miles, this hiking and biking trail meanders within view of the Missouri River for much of the trail's distance across the state. Bikers can enjoy the river as they travel on the longest public portion of the entire Lewis and Clark trail that is not open to motorized traffic.

The solitude, scenery, and small towns along the way make this a popular day trip and weekend destination. Plan to average about eight to twelve miles per hour on your bike. Most cyclists that ride the trail from end to end allow themselves five days for a comfortable trip. Popular Katy Trail trailheads that are rich with Lewis and Clark history include the trail's easternmost trailhead, St. Charles, as well as towns and villages heading west all the way to Boonville, where the trail diverges from the river valley. The Missouri Department of Natural Resources offers an annual organized Katy Trail ride, complete with vehicle support. For more information, visit www.dnr.state.mo.us, or call 800-334-6946.

By Canoe

Paddling the Missouri River will change your view of the river forever. No other river experience allows you the solitude and up-close-and-personal view of the river, and it's as close as most people can get to traveling the river the way Lewis and Clark did. Several communities along the river offer canoe or raft rentals. Only experienced paddlers should tour the river this way, and anyone new to canoeing on the Missouri should be accompanied by someone with experience. First-time paddlers on the Missouri River are often surprised to find that it feels more like a slow-moving lake than a rushing river, but the channel is deep, the current can be unpredictable, and challenges can arise because of debris and other boats.

By Train

Seeing the countryside whirr by while enjoying the comfort and nostalgia of a train is another great way to explore the Lewis and Clark trail on the Missouri River. With stops at several major communities along the river, Amtrak offers a one-of-a-kind way to follow the trail. Special vacation packages and summer rates make this option an affordable experience for the whole family. Visit www.amtrak.com, or call 800-872-7245 for more information. See "Riding the Rails in Missouri," in the June 2003 issue of *Missouri Life* to learn more.

By Bus

For those not looking for a river-based experience, there are also many groups that offer bus tours of the small river towns that dot both banks of the Missouri River. Check your local phone book

Above: Hot-air balloons offer unforgettable views of the Missouri River valley and the surrounding landscape. **Below:** The Army Corps of Engineers maintains a navigation channel on the Missouri River that is three hundred feet wide and nine feet deep.

under "tour operator," or call a local travel agent for information.

By Air

If only Lewis and Clark had such an opportunity to see what lay ahead! Many riverside communities, such as Washington, Missouri, offer short airplane rides that are affordable and offer a chance to experience the river as Lewis and Clark could never have dreamed. The Washington Airport offers rides for about one hundred dollars an hour, which includes a pilot, plane, and seating for two. Appointments are required. For information, call 636-433-5454. Check local listings for other areas.

You can also view the Missouri River from above in a hot-air balloon. Several companies throughout the state offer balloon rides, and prices range from $150-$250 per person for an hour-long ride. Check local listings for information. See "Into the Blue Yonder: Where to Get Balloon Rides," in the August 2002 issue of *Missouri Life* to learn more.

ABOUT THE AUTHOR: **Brett Dufur** is the author of *The Complete Katy Trail Guidebook*. He has also explored the Missouri River as a member of the Discovery Expedition of St. Charles. *(See page 40.)* Brett's new book, *Exploring Lewis & Clark's Missouri,* was recently released by Pebble Publishing.

Travelers on the Missouri River today can experience the same dramatic sunsets and serene settings that Lewis and Clark enjoyed two hundred years ago.

ALONG THE RIVER WITH LEWIS AND CLARK

THE CORPS OF DISCOVERY spent more than two hundred days in Missouri during its voyage westward and its return trip. Along the Missouri River, the explorers observed vast prairies, lush forests, huge herds of deer, and fertile riverbanks. The men were challenged by rough stretches of river and dangerous snags that threatened and occasionally damaged the boats. They endured mosquitoes, ticks, heavy rains, and sometimes oppressive heat, and they also enjoyed gentle breezes, beautiful scenery, and spectacular sunsets. Lewis and Clark were impressed by the land they traveled through and the people they met in Missouri, and they dutifully recorded the details of their experience in their expedition journals.

On the following pages, you'll discover the Missouri that Lewis and Clark knew, and you'll learn about their day-by-day experience through their own words, with details and descriptions taken directly from their journals. Seven one-of-a-kind maps created by geographer Jim Harlan let you track the expedition's route through the state, and stunning photographs depict the Missouri River as Lewis and Clark might have seen it.

Information about historic sites, state parks, charming river towns, and other points of interest will help you plan your own expedition along Lewis and Clark's route, which includes what is now the Katy Trail, Missouri's wine country, sites of Civil War battles, and plenty of opportunities for scenic views of the Missouri River. >>>

[FALL 1803]

FROM SOUTHEASTERN MISSOURI TO ST. LOUIS

Southeastern Missouri, at the confluence of the Ohio and Mississippi Rivers
November 20, 1803

The Corps of Discovery begins its ascent of the Mississippi River. All journal entries from this point to November 28 are made by Lewis.

Visit Fort Massac State Park
Metropolis, Illinois

Overlooking the Ohio River from the southern tip of Illinois, the 1,450-acre Fort Massac became Illinois's first state park in 1908. The French built Fort De L'Ascension on the site in 1757, during the French and Indian War, and since then, the fort has been destroyed or dismantled and rebuilt several times. Today, a replica of a timber structure built in 1794 stands on the site. Lewis hired the Corps of Discovery's interpreter, George Drouillard, here.
dnr.state.il.us/lands/landmgt/
PARKS/R5/frmindex.htm
618-524-4712

Near Commerce, Missouri
November 22, 1803

The men set out early on a rapid and difficult current. Lewis kills a heath hen to make soup for Clark, who has been ill for nearly a week. They see part of an American settlement of about fifteen families in an area called Tywappity Bottom. About twenty-two miles above the junction with the Ohio River, the men overtake two keelboats from Louisville, Kentucky, that are loaded with dry goods and whiskey and bound for Kaskaskia, on the Illinois side. Lewis records seeing poplar and white oak, and he describes the tallest scouring rush plant he has ever seen — more than eight feet high and three inches in circumference. Lewis notes that the plant remains hardy through the winter and is healthy food for horses and cattle. After the men camp on the eastern shore, crew member Nathaniel Pryor goes

out to hunt, but he does not return. To bring him in, the men fire guns and blow a horn to no avail.

Cape Girardeau, Missouri
November 23, 1803

Pryor still has not returned. The men fire guns and blow the horn again, and then they leave without him. They pass Cape La Croix Creek, land at Cape Girardeau, and meet the commandant there, Louis Lorimier. Lewis attends a horse race with Lorimier and his family. In a dispute involving a wager, Lorimier loses four horses worth two hundred dollars. The scene reminds Lewis of uncivilized backwoodsmen in Kentucky. He writes, "it is not extrawdinary that these people should be disorderly they are almost entirely emigrant from the fronteers of Kentuckey and Tennessee, and are the most dessolute and abandoned even among these people; they are men of desperate fortunes, but little to loose either character or property — they bett very high on these raises in proportion to their wealth. ..."

Visit the Site of Lorimier's Red House
South Main and William Streets
Louis Lorimier, who is credited with founding Cape Girardeau, came to the area in 1793 after being commissioned by the Spanish to establish a military post for trade

and interaction with American Indians. His home, known as the Red House, was on the site of the present Old St. Vincent's Church.

Near Neely's Landing, Missouri
November 24, 1803

As the explorers set out in the morning, they are hailed by Pryor, who is ill and fatigued after being lost for two days. Lewis observes limestone rocks embedded with chunks of smooth chert.

Visit Trail of Tears State Park
429 Moccasin Springs
Jackson, Missouri

This 3,415-acre park offers a spectacular view of the Mississippi River and stands as a memorial to the Cherokee Indians who lost their lives during the forced relocation in the harsh winter of 1838-39. Nine of thirteen groups of relocated Cherokees crossed the Mississippi River at this point.
www.mostateparks.com/trailoftears.htm
800-334-6946

Near Wittenberg, Missouri
November 25, 1803

The men come to Apple Creek, which Lewis describes as "the most considerable stream I have yet met with." They arrive at Grand Tower (now known as Tower Rock) just before sunset, and they camp on the Missouri shore.

Above, from left: Relocated Cherokees crossed the Mississippi River at the site of Trail of Tears State Park. The Museum of Westward Expansion displays Indian exhibits and artifacts.

On the Mississippi River, north of Cape Girardeau, November 25, 1803
"Arrived at the Grand Tower a little before sunset, passed above it and came too on the Lard. shore for the night. ... This seems among the watermen of the mississippi to be what the tropics or Equanoxial line is with regard to the Sailors; those who have never passed it before are always compelled to pay or furnish some sperits to drink or be ducked." — Meriwether Lewis

ALONG THE RIVER [FALL 1803]

side of the river. A quarter mile away is Cinque Hommes Creek, which is twenty miles long and home to a considerable number of settlers and as many as three grist mills.

Visit Seventy-six Conservation Area

Seven miles south of Perryville off of Highway 61 *Seventy-six Conservation Area covers 818 acres of forest and borders a two-mile section of the Mississippi River.*

Near Ste. Genevieve, Missouri
November 28, 1803

Lewis leaves Clark in charge of the boat. Clark and the men set out from Horse Island, opposite Kaskaskia River. A foggy morning obscures the shore's view. They pass Donohoe's Landing on the Missouri side, where boats receive salt from the nearby saline licks that would make Ste. Genevieve prosperous. They pass the mouth of the Saline Creek, which has a "thick settlement" of pioneers on its banks. After passing swift water between sandbars, they arrive at a landing on the Illinois side known as Kaskaskia, a community of about 467 people.

Visit Ste. Genevieve, Missouri

"Ste. Gen" was founded in 1735 by French Canadians. Many sites are open to visitors and offer a unique look into Missouri's French past.
www.saintegenevievetourism.org
800-373-7007

Grand Tower
November 26, 1803

Lewis climbs this limestone formation and drops a cord from the top to determine that it is ninety-two feet high. On the Missouri side, a high point of land topped by a conical formation known as a sugar loaf looks down on the tower and affords a view of the river. Another large rock, 120 yards in circumference and forty feet high, is located in the river three hundred yards from this point. Lewis speculates that these outcroppings were part of a ridge of hills that were two hundred feet high and eroded over time. He notes that when the river is high, a powerful whirlpool forms between the Grand Tower and a nearby rock formation.

Visit Tower Rock Natural Area

Take Highway 61 to Uniontown, and go east on Route A to the river

When Lewis and Clark passed by Tower Rock in 1803, Lewis reported that the rock was thought of as a great divide, like passing the equator. Today, sightseers can walk on flat rocks near river level or climb a bluff near Tower Rock for better views.

Near Chester, Illinois
November 27, 1803

The Corps of Discovery sets out before sunrise and proceeds to a point of rocks on the edge of a long range of hills on the Missouri

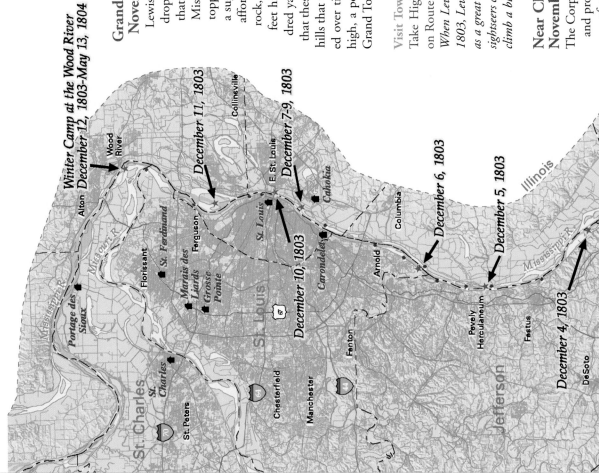

Winter Camp at the Wood River
December 12, 1803-May 13, 1804

December 11, 1803

December 7-9, 1803

December 10, 1803

December 6, 1803

December 5, 1803

December 4, 1803

St. Charles

St. Louis

Jefferson

Illinois

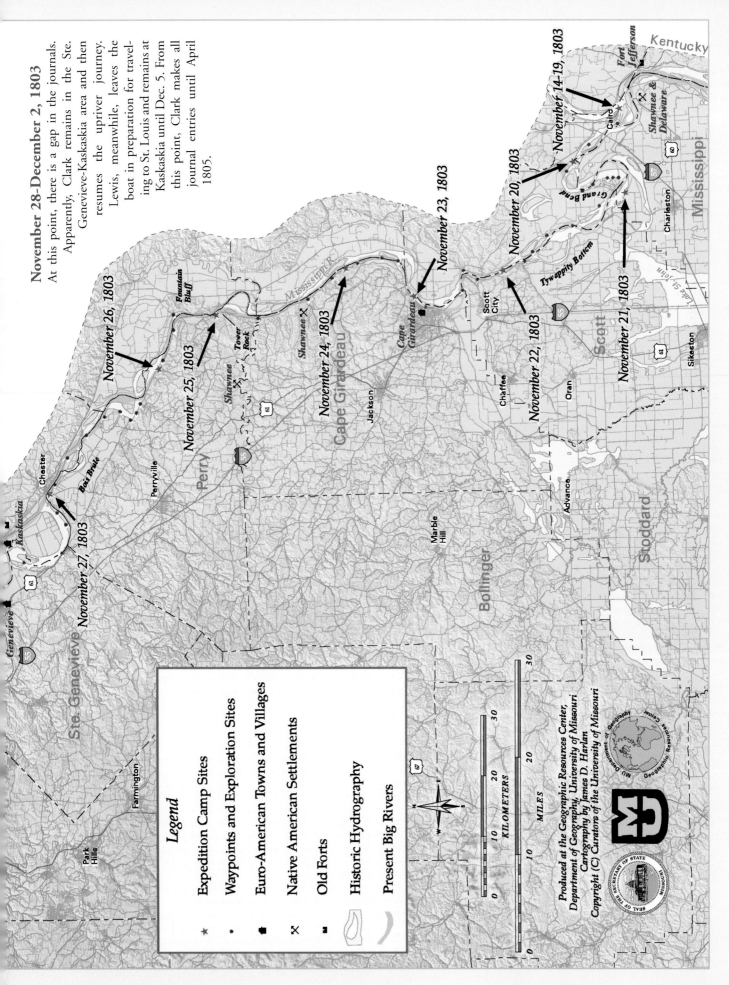

November 28-December 2, 1803

At this point, there is a gap in the journals. Apparently, Clark remains in the Ste. Genevieve-Kaskaskia area and then resumes the upriver journey. Lewis, meanwhile, leaves the boat in preparation for traveling to St. Louis and remains at Kaskaskia until Dec. 5. From this point, Clark makes all journal entries until April 1805.

November 27, 1803

November 26, 1803

November 25, 1803

November 24, 1803

November 23, 1803

November 22, 1803

November 21, 1803

November 20, 1803

November 14-19, 1803

Legend

Expedition Camp Sites

Waypoints and Exploration Sites

Euro-American Towns and Villages

Native American Settlements

Old Forts

Historic Hydrography

Present Big Rivers

Produced at the Geographic Resource Center,
Department of Geography, University of Missouri
Cartography by James D. Harlan
Copyright (C) Curators of the University of Missouri

KILOMETERS

MILES

Kentucky

Mississippi

Stoddard

Scott

Bollinger

Perry

Ste. Genevieve

Kaskaskia

Genevieve

Chester

Boat Brale

Perryville

Fountain Bluff

Tower Rock

Shawnee

Shawnee

Jackson

Cape Girardeau

Chaffee

Scott City

Oran

Advance

Marble Hill

Farmington

Park Hills

Fort Jefferson

Cairo

Shawnee & Delaware

Grand Bend

Tywappity Bottom

Charleston

Sikeston

Lake St. John

December 3-4, 1803

Clark and his men leave before sunrise and come to the Missouri shore after dark. The next day, they pass Gabourie Creek at the mouth of a landing for trading boats of Ste. Genevieve, a small town that is situated on the spurs of the highland and is home to about 120 families who are mostly French. The men press on and see a cave twelve feet in diameter and seventy feet above the water. They pass the site of Old Fort De Chartres. Clark writes, "The chanel which forms the Island next to the fort is intirely dry, and appears to be filling up with sand and mud, the River at this place is wide, and remarkably Streight. …"

Visit Fort De Chartres
1350 State Route 155
Prairie du Rocher, Illinois
Built in 1720, this was the center of French civil and military government in the Illinois area during the eighteenth century. The French held the garrison until October 1765, when English troops replaced them in accordance with the treaty that ended the French and Indian War. In 1772, the British

destroyed the fort. The park includes a reconstruction of the third fort built on this site.
www.state.il.us/hpa/hs/DeChartres.htm
618-284-7230

Near Crystal City, Missouri
December 5, 1803

Clark and his men see caves and indented arches in the cliffs on the Missouri side. They pass Platten Creek, with dense settlements of Americans. They dine at a creek with a rock that forms a natural two-hundred-foot wharf. On the Illinois side, they come to Eagle Creek. They intend to land here to take in provisions, but none have arrived. They proceed a half mile above the landing and camp for the night.

Near Arnold, Missouri
December 6, 1803

On this dark, wet morning, Clark learns that Lewis passed through the day before on his way to St. Louis. Clark and his men pass by several creeks, small islands, and some swift water. When the men pass Little Rock Creek, Clark notices several settlements. They also pass the mouth of the Meramec River.

Near Cahokia, Missouri
December 7, 1803

The wind becomes so violent on this day that it blows one of the masts off. The men pass a village at the mouth of a large creek called the River Des Peres, about four miles south of St. Louis. This village, Carondelet, is nicknamed *Vide Poche*, which means "empty pocket" in French, and it contains a number of French families. In the afternoon, the men come to Cahokia Landing, at the mouth of Cahokia Creek.

December 8-10, 1803

There are no journal entries from these days. The men remain at Cahokia, and Lewis joins them after meeting with Spanish Lieutenant Governor Carlos Dehault Delassus, who denies permission to ascend the Missouri until he gets approval from his superiors. Lewis is not worried, as he knows the party plans to winter at Wood River, and the territory will be transferred to the United States soon, when the Louisiana Purchase is finalized.

On Gabaret Island, Illinois
December 11, 1803

On this rainy morning, the men cross the river to St. Louis. Lewis remains to acquire information about the country and to prepare dispatches to be mailed to the government. The men then move on in the rain and camp on the side of a large island on the Illinois side. The current is against the Missouri shore, and the banks are falling in where there is no rock.

Near Alton, Illinois
December 12, 1803

The men set out after a night of heavy northwestern winds. On the Missouri side, there is a settlement in a small prairie, perhaps the village of St. Ferdinand, present-day Florissant. They come to the mouth of the Wood River as the winds increase to a full-fledged storm with hail and snow. After landing, they see two canoes of Potawatomi Indians land on the opposite bank. Three of the Potawatomi men come across the river in a canoe and tell Clark that the country is beautiful and has plenty of game.

Visit Wood River Museum and Visitor's Center
40 West Ferguson Avenue
Wood River, Illinois
The site includes a model of the Corps of Discovery's Camp DuBois. A replica of the camp, where Lewis and Clark spent the winter of 1803-04, is being built at the intersection of Route 143 and Route 3 in Wood River.
www.woodriver.org/Community/Museum
618-254-1993

Visit the Lewis and Clark Interpretive Center
1 Lewis and Clark Trail
Hartford, Illinois
One of the premier Lewis and Clark sites in America, this fourteen-thousand-square-foot exhibit offers displays and multimedia presentations on the expedition, including a full-size cutaway keelboat, a replica of the Corps of Discovery's fifty-five-foot vessel that is open on one side to reveal hidden interior passages, storage compartments, living quarters, and cargo.
www.state.il.us/hpa/LewClark.htm
618-251-5811

Visit the Museum of Westward Expansion
Beneath the Gateway Arch
St. Louis, Missouri
Explore the history of American westward movement with murals depicting scenes along Lewis and Clark's route, descriptions from their journals, life-sized animatronic figures of Lewis, Clark, and American Indians, and the world's largest collection of American Indian peace medals.
www.nps.gov/jeff/mus-tour.htm
314-655-1700

Visit St. Louis's Old Courthouse
Two blocks west of the Gateway Arch
St. Louis, Missouri
View a film that explains the role of St. Louis in the history of the United States, and see a diorama depicting the ceremony of the transfer of the Upper Louisiana Territory, which both Lewis and Clark attended.
www.nps.gov/jeff/och.htm
314-655-1700

Visit the Missouri History Museum
Lindell and DeBaliviere at Forest Park
St. Louis, Missouri
See Clark's journal and other artifacts in an extensive Lewis and Clark collection. The museum was chosen to host a major exhibit mounted by the Missouri Historical Society from January 14 to September 6, 2004. (See pages 44 to 48.) The six-thousand-square-foot exhibit includes more than five hundred artifacts and documents — many from the families of Lewis and Clark — that have not been seen in one place since 1806.
www.mohistory.org
314-454-3124

Visit Bellefontaine Cemetery
4947 West Florissant
St. Louis, Missouri
The site of Clark's grave includes a granite obelisk and a bust of the explorer that reads, "Soldier, Explorer, Statesman and Patriot. His Life is Written in the History of His Country."
314-381-0750

Visit Jefferson Barracks
533 Grant Road
St. Louis, Missouri
Once the largest military post in the United States, Jefferson Barracks sits on the original site of Fort Bellefontaine, the first U.S. military post located in the Louisiana Purchase. See "Jefferson Barracks" in the December 2002 issue of Missouri Life to learn more.
www.stlouisco.com/parks/j-b.html
314-544-5714

From left: Jefferson Barracks Historic Site at St. Louis offers a winter view of the Mississippi River. The sun sets on the serene Missouri River near Marion.

[SPRING 1804]
FROM ST. LOUIS TO WASHINGTON

Eastern Missouri, at the confluence of the Missouri and Mississippi Rivers
May 14, 1804

On this cloudy morning, William Clark and his men begin their ascent of the Missouri River from their winter camp at Wood River, known then as the River Dubois. They travel four and one-half miles and then camp on an island near Coldwater Creek. Meriwether Lewis remains at St. Louis to take care of last-minute affairs and eventually joins Clark at St. Charles. There has been some debate over the Corps of Discovery's official departure point. Some say St. Louis was the explorers' Gateway to the West, while others assert that the journey officially began when Lewis joined Clark at St. Charles and they set out together with their Corps of Discovery. In his journal, Lewis writes: "The mouth of the River Dubois is to be considered as the point of departure."

Visit Columbia Bottom Conservation Area

In northern St. Louis County, about 2.5 miles north of the Interstate 270 Riverview Drive exit
This 4,318-acre area offers a front-row seat to view the confluence of the Missouri and Mississippi Rivers, as well as ongoing conservation efforts and recreational opportunities.
www.conservation.state.mo.us
636-441-4554

Visit Pelican Island Natural Area

In northern St. Louis County, on the Missouri River
This 2,260-acre area is accessible only to boaters. The site preserves one of the best remaining examples of what the islands on the lower Missouri River looked like before it was channelized, and it features a bottomland forest, shifting sandbars, and mudflats.
www.conservation.state.mo.us
636-441-4554

Near Black Walnut, Missouri
May 15, 1804

After traveling nine and one-half miles, the men camp on the north shore at Piper's Landing. A heavily laden stern causes the keelboat to become stuck on logs in the water three times. Clark notes that one of the pirogues is undermanned and has trouble keeping up. He writes of passing a site called the Plattes, where he sees a flat rock projecting from the foot of a hill.

Visit St. Stanislaus Conservation Area

From St. Louis, take Route 370 to Earth City Expressway and travel 3.5 miles north
This 810-acre area is named for the St. Stanislaus Seminary, which was once located here. For a view of the Missouri River bottoms, visitors can hike to a bluff that early French explorers named La Charbonier, or "coal seam." Lewis and Clark noted the area's coal resources when they passed by the spot.
www.conservation.state.mo.us
636-441-4554

St. Charles, Missouri
May 16-21, 1804

Clark arrives on May 16 with the keelboat, two pirogues, and about forty men. He notes that the village of St. Charles is about one mile in length and consists of about 450 people who are primarily French. The village was founded as *Les Petites Cotes,* which means "the little hills," and the Spanish knew it as *San Carlos del Misuri.* While waiting for Lewis to arrive, the men make final purchases and enjoy the hospitality of the inhabitants. Residents invite the men to dinners, a dance, and a church service. This will be their last visit to an established town for more than two years. On May 17, three crew members are court-martialed for being absent without leave. One of them, John Collins, is also charged with behaving in an unbecoming manner at a ball and using disrespectful language. Collins is found guilty and sentenced to "fifty lashes

From top: Travelers can follow Lewis and Clark by walking or biking along the scenic Katy Trail. Main Street at St. Charles is Missouri's largest historic district.

on his naked back." The other men, William Warner and Hugh Hall, are granted leniency. Lewis arrives in St. Charles on May 20 with some well-wishers from St. Louis. The next day, Clark writes: "Set out from St. Charles at three oClock after getting every matter arranged, proceeded on under a jentle Breese." Foul weather sets in a mile upriver, and the men only travel about four miles before they set up camp on the first island. It rains "powerfully" through the night.

Visit St. Charles, Missouri
Main Street at St. Charles is the largest his-

On the Missouri River, east of Washington, Missouri, May 24, 1804

"Set out early passed a Verry bad part of the River Called the Deavels race ground. … passed Several Islands, two Small Creeks … we attempted to pass up under the Lbd. Bank which was falling in So fast that the evident danger obliged us to Cross between the Starbd. Side and a Sand bar, the Sand moveing & banking caused us to run on the Sand. The Swiftness of the Current wheeled the boat, Broke our Toe rope, and was nearly over Setting the boat, all hand Jumped out on the upper Side and bore on that Side untill the Sand washed from under the boat and wheeled on the next bank by the time She wheeled a 3rd Time got a rope fast to her Stern and by the means of Swimmers was Carred to Shore and when her Stern was down whilst in the act of Swinging a third time into Deep water near the Shore. … we Camped about 1 mile above where we were So nearly being lost. … on a Plantation. all in Spirits. This place I call the retragrade bend as we were obliged to fall back 2 miles." — William Clark

toric district in Missouri, and it includes 125 craft and specialty shops. Visitors can explore Missouri's first state capitol and see where the Corps of Discovery set out on the Missouri River at what is now Frontier Park. The annual Lewis and Clark Heritage Days are held the third weekend of each May. The Lewis and Clark Center features exhibits on the expedition, and visitors can view replicas of the explorers' keelboat and two pirogues.
www.historicstcharles.com
800-366-2427

Visit Katy Trail State Park

Much of Lewis and Clark's trip across Missouri can be traveled by following the Katy Trail, a former railroad right-of-way that was converted into a 225-mile bike path. The trail winds along the Missouri River from St. Charles to Boonville and then veers away from the river to Clinton. It passes through historic towns that feature local wineries, bed and breakfasts, and campgrounds. The trail's flat gravel surface makes it easy to follow in Lewis and Clark's footsteps, and bikes can be rented along the trail.
www.katytrailstatepark.com
800-334-6946

Visit August A. Busch Memorial Conservation Area

2360 Highway D
near St. Charles, Missouri
This sixty-nine-hundred-acre area is great for bird-watching, hiking, and fishing on the site's thirty-two small lakes. Visitors can also enjoy an eight-mile driving tour of the area.
www.conservation.state.mo.us
636-441-4554

Visit Weldon Spring Conservation Area

Just south of August A. Busch Memorial Conservation Area
This seventy-three-hundred-acre site offers hiking, mountain-biking trails, and roads that lead to the Missouri River for scenic views.
www.conservation.state.mo.us
636-441-4554

Near Weldon Spring, Missouri
May 22, 1804

The Corps of Discovery sets out on a cloudy morning and passes several small farms, Bonhomme Creek, and a camp of Kickapoo Indians. Clark writes, "Those Indians told me Several days ago that they would Come on & hunt and by the time I got to their

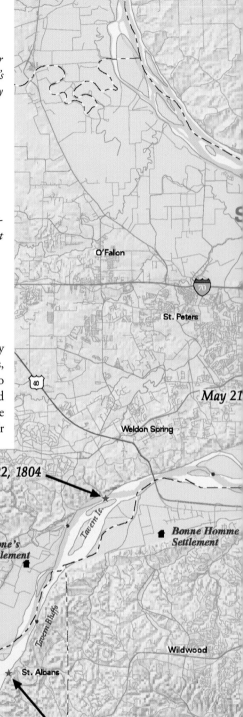

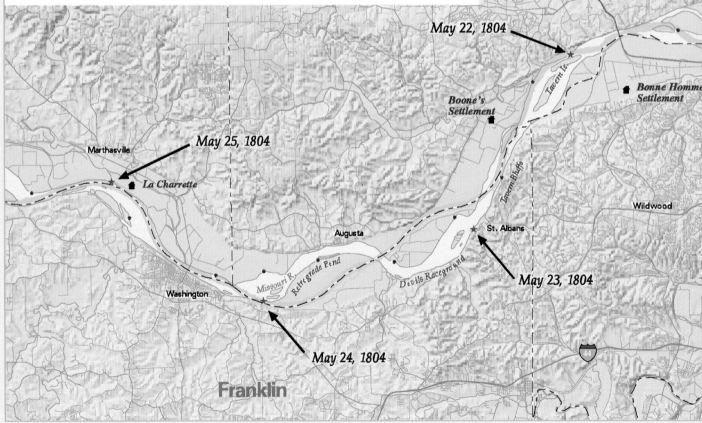

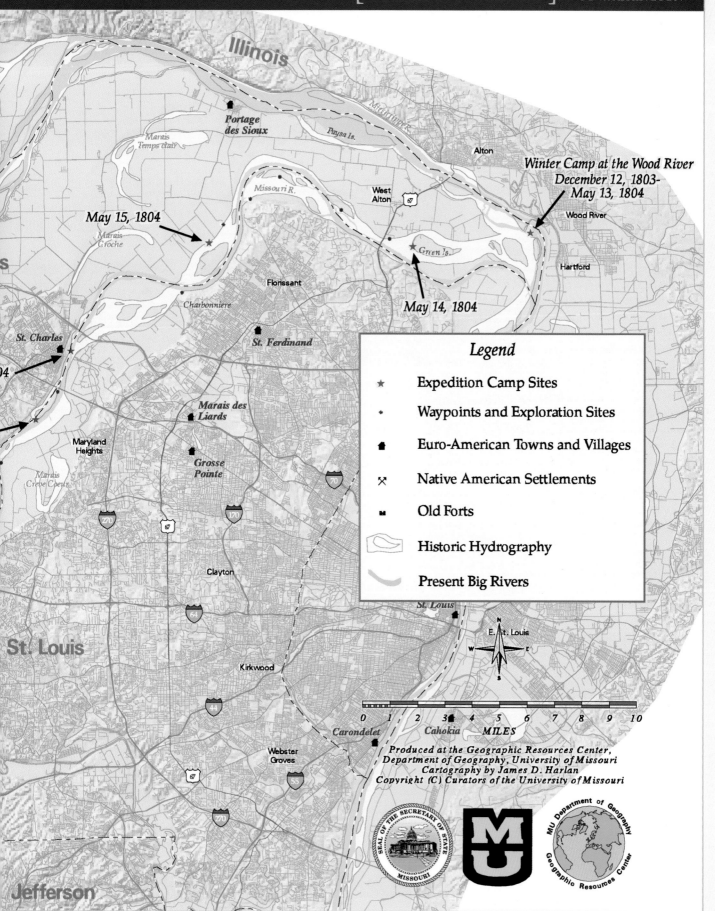

Illinois

Portage
des Sioux

Marais
Temps clair

Paysa Is.

Mississippi

Alton

Missouri R.

West
Alton

Winter Camp at the Wood River
December 12, 1803-
May 13, 1804

Wood River

May 15, 1804

Marais
Croche

Green Is.

Hartford

Florissant

Charbonniere

May 14, 1804

St. Charles

St. Ferdinand

04

Legend

⭐ Expedition Camp Sites

✦ Waypoints and Exploration Sites

⌂ Euro-American Towns and Villages

⚒ Native American Settlements

⊟ Old Forts

Historic Hydrography

Present Big Rivers

Marais des
Liards

Maryland
Heights

Marais
Creve Coeur

Grosse
Pointe

St. Louis

E. St. Louis

N
W   E
S

Clayton

St. Louis

Kirkwood

0 1 2 3 4 5 6 7 8 9 10
MILES

Carondelet

Cahokia

Webster
Groves

Produced at the Geographic Resources Center,
Department of Geography, University of Missouri
Cartography by James D. Harlan
Copyright (C) Curators of the University of Missouri

SEAL OF THE SECRETARY OF STATE
MISSOURI

MU

MU Department of Geography
Geographic Resources Center

Jefferson

Camp they would have Some Provisions for us. …" The men camp at a bend in the river, and the Indians arrive with a gift of four deer. The men offer two quarts of whiskey in exchange.

Near St. Albans, Missouri
May 23, 1804

After running into a log, the men are delayed for an hour. They then pass Femme Osage Creek, where there is an American settlement of thirty or forty families. After leaving the keelboat and crew to get a better view of nearby Tavern Cave, Lewis scrambles up the bluff to survey the country ahead. He slips and almost falls several hundred feet before driving a knife into loose rock and soil to stop his fall. Clark writes: "we passed a large Cave … (called by the french the Tavern) about 120 feet wide 40 feet Deep & 20 feet high many different immages are Painted on the Rock at this place. The Inds. & French pay omage. many nams are wrote on the rock, Stoped about one mile above for Capt Lewis who had assended the Clifts. … Capt. Lewis near falling from the … rocks 300 feet, he caught at 20 foot."

Visit Daniel Boone Home & Boonesfield Village
1868 Highway F
Defiance, Missouri
Daniel Boone spent his last living days on this site, at a picturesque four-story home that was built in the early 1800s. Structures around the home reflect the time of the Louisiana Purchase and the early days of Missouri's statehood. Boonesfield Village, a replica of an early community, offers a living-history experience throughout the year.
www.lindenwood.edu
636-798-2005

Visit Augusta, Missouri
Located in the heart of Missouri's Weinstrasse (wine road) region, this quaint river town was founded as Mount Pleasant in 1836, but its name was later changed. The town is now known primarily as an antiques, shopping, bed-and-breakfast, and wine destination.
www.augusta-missouri.com
636-482-4000

Visit Shaw Nature Reserve
Gray Summit, Missouri
The twenty-five-hundred-acre Shaw Nature Reserve includes fourteen miles of hiking trails through wetlands, upland and bottomland forest, glades, and tallgrass prairie. An eight-acre wildflower garden features native plants, and the Bascom House, built in 1879, includes exhibits about the environment.
www.mobot.org/mobot/naturereserve/
636-451-3512

Near Washington, Missouri
May 24, 1804

The crew passes a half-mile of projecting

From top: The view from Tavern Rock, near St. Albans, where Lewis almost fell to his death. Washington, Missouri, sits right on the Missouri River.

rocks called the Devil's race ground, known today as Liffecue Rocks. Progress is delayed when a strong current catches the keelboat as it passes a sandbar. The current is so strong that it breaks the towrope and causes the boat to turn end to end three times before it finally comes to rest in deep water. In one of three different journal entries describing this experience, Clark writes, "this place being the worst I ever Saw, I call it the retregrade bend." Despite these troubles, the boats make ten miles of progress.

Visit Washington, Missouri
Washington traces its roots back to the early 1820s, when it served as a ferry landing, and later as a steamboat landing, on the Missouri River. The area was settled by followers of Daniel Boone and early German immigrants. In 1855, John Busch, the older brother of Adolphus Busch, started a brewery here that bottled the original Busch Beer. The area includes numerous wineries, a historic downtown, the only factory in the world that still manufactures corncob pipes, and the Gary R. Lucy Gallery at 231 West Main Street, which features paintings by Gary Lucy that were inspired by the Lewis and Clark expedition.
www.washmo.org
888-792-7466

[SUMMER 1804]

FROM WASHINGTON TO NORTHWESTERN MISSOURI

Near Marthasville, Missouri
May 25, 1804

After spending another rainy night on the Missouri River, the Corps of Discovery travels ten miles, passing several small creeks, an island, and then camping at the mouth of a creek near the small French village of La Charrette. There are seven families living here, and it is the westernmost white settlement that the Corps of Discovery will encounter. Clark writes "The people at this Village is pore, houses Small, they Sent us milk & eggs to eat."

Visit Marthasville, Missouri

Marthasville is a Katy Trail biker's oasis. Several cafes and bed and breakfasts offer modern-day explorers a respite that Lewis and Clark would surely have enjoyed. Daniel Boone's arrival in the area in 1799 was a signal of American westward expansion, and after the Louisiana Purchase in 1803, French settlers began selling their claims to Americans. The French settlement that had been here became an American settlement when Dr. John Young founded a town on higher ground nearby and named it for his wife, Martha.
636-433-5242

Visit New Haven, Missouri

New Haven is a picture-perfect river town that offers food, lodging, and a nice vantage point to photograph the Missouri River. A nearby boat ramp, Colter's Landing, is named for Corps of Discovery member Private John

Colter. After the expedition, he traveled back up the Missouri River and into the Northern Rockies. He remained there for six years and is thought to be the first white man to see what would later become Yellowstone National Park, referred to at the time as "Colter's Hell" because of Colter's descriptions of the geysers and hot springs he saw there. Colter later married and settled in Missouri, where he died of jaundice in his thirties, in 1813.
573-237-3830

Near Berger, Missouri
May 26, 1804

The men set out this morning after a heavy rain. A stiff wind allows them to "proceed on verry well under Sale," which was not common for them on the lower Missouri. The captains direct George Drouillard and John Shields to proceed ahead for one day and hunt the next before meeting up with the boats again. The rest of the men camp on an island below Loutre Island, which means "otter" island in French. Lewis and Clark organize twenty-six of the men into three squads under the command of Sergeants Floyd, Ordway, and Pryor. The remaining men are divided into two groups: seven engagés under Patroon (foreman) Jean Baptiste Dechamps and six privates under Cpl. Richard Warfington.

Visit Graham Cave State Park

217 Highway TT
Montgomery City, Missouri
Located about twenty miles north of the

Missouri River, this 356-acre site includes a cave that was used by humans as far back as ten thousand years ago. The forested area also includes trails, boating on the Loutre River, and camping facilities.
www.mostateparks.com/grahamcave.htm
800-334-6946

Visit Hermann, Missouri

This historic German community, founded in 1836, includes several wineries, including Stone Hill Winery, the state's largest. Visitors can choose from many bed and breakfasts and restaurants, and the large historic district includes well-preserved examples of the state's early German architecture.
www.hermannmo.com
800-932-8687

Near Gasconade, Missouri
May 27-28, 1804

This morning, the explorers encounter two canoes floating downstream loaded with beaver, elk, deer skins, and buffalo robes from the Omaha nation. They later encounter four rafts loaded with furs and pelts from the Pawnees and Grand Osages. After traveling about fifteen miles, they camp at the mouth of the Gasconade River, and George Shannon kills a deer. After a night of hard rain, the men find that many of their things have gotten wet, and some tobacco has spoiled. The wet items are set out to dry. Clark notes that the sky is cloudy and that the river has begun to rise quickly.

Above from left: Hermann offers several wineries, a historic courthouse, and peaceful views of the Missouri River. Lush greenery spreads across the river valley at Marion Bottoms, northwest of Jefferson City. The Dauphine Hotel at Bonnots Mill was built around 1875.

On the Missouri River, near Easley, Missouri, June 5, 1804

"after Jurking the meet Killed yesterday and Crossing the hunting party we Set out at 6 oClock. ... at 11 oClock brought too a Small Caissee in which was two french men, from 80 Leagues up the Kansias R. where they wintered and Cought a great quantity of Beaver, the greater part of which they lost by fire from the Praries, those men inform that the Kansas Nation are now out in the plains hunting Buffalow. ... Passed a projecting rock on which was painted a figue and a Creek at 2 ms above Called Little Manitou Creek from the Painted rock. ... passed a Small Creek on L. S. opposit a Verry bad Sand bar of Several ms. in extent, which we named Sand C here my Servant York Swam to the Sand bar to geather greens for our Dinner. ... the Watr. uncertain the quick Sand Moveing we had a fine wind but could not make use of it, our Mast being broke. ... our Scout discovd. the fresh sign of about 10 Inds. I expect that those Indians are on their way to war against the Osages nation probably they are Saukees." — William Clark

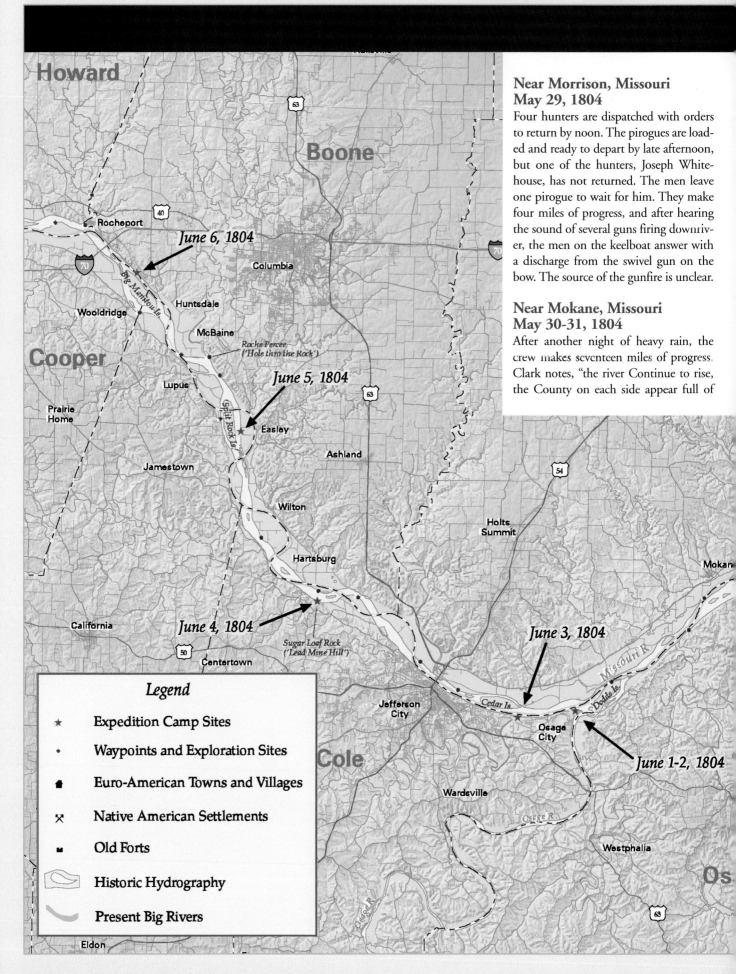

Howard

Boone

Rocheport

June 6, 1804

Columbia

Huntsdale

Wooldridge

McBaine

Roche Percee ('Hole thro the Rock')

Cooper

Lupus

June 5, 1804

Easley

Prairie Home

Ashland

Jamestown

Wilton

Holts Summit

Hartsburg

California

June 4, 1804

Sugar Loaf Rock ('Lead Mine Hill')

Centertown

June 3, 1804

Mokan

Jefferson City

Cole

Cedar Is.

Osage City

Dodds Is.

June 1-2, 1804

Wardsville

Osage R.

Westphalia

Os

Eldon

Legend

★   Expedition Camp Sites

•   Waypoints and Exploration Sites

▲   Euro-American Towns and Villages

✗   Native American Settlements

⊾   Old Forts

〰   Historic Hydrography

〰   Present Big Rivers

Near Morrison, Missouri
May 29, 1804
Four hunters are dispatched with orders to return by noon. The pirogues are loaded and ready to depart by late afternoon, but one of the hunters, Joseph Whitehouse, has not returned. The men leave one pirogue to wait for him. They make four miles of progress, and after hearing the sound of several guns firing downriver, the men on the keelboat answer with a discharge from the swivel gun on the bow. The source of the gunfire is unclear.

Near Mokane, Missouri
May 30-31, 1804
After another night of heavy rain, the crew makes seventeen miles of progress. Clark notes, "the river Continue to rise, the County on each side appear full of

Water." The men camp at the mouth of Grindstone Creek. The next day, Clark talks with a French trader and an Indian woman who are heading downriver. They have come from trading with the Grand Osage Indians on the Arkansas River. They tell the captains that a letter that had been delivered to the Grand Osages explaining that the United States now controlled their land had been "Commited to the flaims." In his journal, Clark writes, "Several rats of Considerable Size was Cought in the woods to day." These were likely eastern wood rats, a species new to American science at the time.

Visit Bonnots Mill, Missouri
This small river town of about two hundred people, hemmed in by steep hills and bluffs, offers a nice reward for taking the back roads:

the historic Dauphine Hotel, a restaurant, and nice views of the Missouri River.

Near Osage City, Missouri
June 1-2, 1804
The men encounter swift water and falling banks on the river. George Drouillard and John Shields return "much worsted" after being gone for seven days.

Near Wainwright, Missouri
June 3, 1804
The men make five miles of progress today and camp at the mouth of the Moreau River. In his journal, Clark complains of a sore throat and says he is also "Tormented with Musquetors & Small ticks."

Visit Jefferson City, Missouri
At Missouri's capital city, tour the Jefferson

Landing Historic Site, where steamboats brought immigrants who settled the area. Visitors can also tour the state capitol, which features murals by Thomas Hart Benton and several tributes to the Corps of Discovery expedition, including a statue of Thomas Jefferson. www.visitjeffersoncity.com
573-632-2820

Near Hartsburg, Missouri
June 4, 1804
The voyagers pass Cedar Island and a small creek that they "named Nightingale Creek from a Bird of that discription which Sang for us all last night." After traveling about seven miles, the keelboat's mast breaks after the boat passes under a bent tree. During a daytime stop, Clark explores an area in what is today northern Cole County. He ascends a hill 170 feet high and finds a large mound,

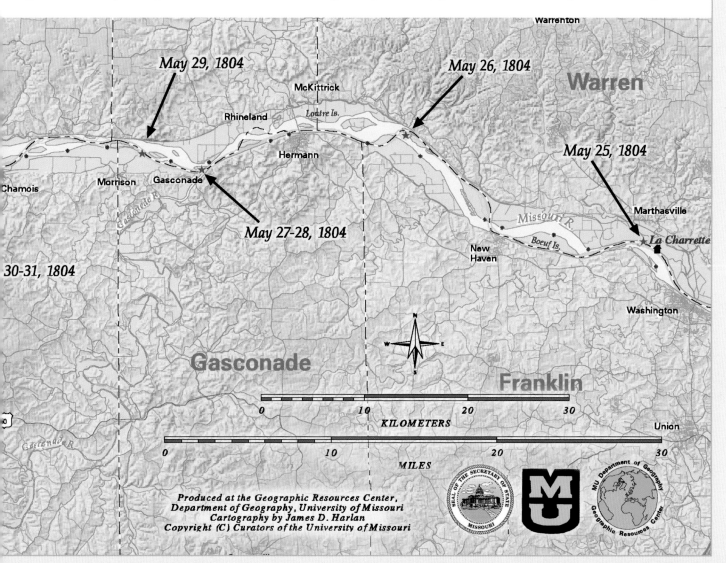

Produced at the Geographic Resources Center, Department of Geography, University of Missouri Cartography by James D. Harlan Copyright (C) Curators of the University of Missouri

a hundred acres of dead trees, and a cave. On a rock projecting over the river (Sugar Loaf Rock), he enjoys an unencumbered view of the river for more than twenty miles. Hunters kill seven deer today, and the crew proceeds more than seventeen miles.

Visit Wilton, Missouri

This tiny river hamlet is known for the Riverview Traders Store, which offers cabins and the only camping spot on the entire Katy Trail where you can spend the night in a tepee.
573-657-1095

Near Easley, Missouri
June 5, 1804

The men jerk the venison killed the day before by cutting it into strips and drying it in the sun. They meet two Frenchmen coming from the Kansas River. Two miles above Moniteau Creek, they pass a projecting rock with a figure painted on it, which Clark calls a "Deavel." York swims to an island to gather greens, and the hunters discover the signs of a war party, which Clark says are probably the "Saukees" on their way to war against the Osages. The current makes moving upriver difficult, but the boats make more than twelve miles of progress. Clark notes that he is "verry unwell with a Slight feever. …"

Visit Cooper's Landing
Cooper's Landing, just upriver from Easley, hosts live music during the summer, and it is

the only place in mid-Missouri to refuel your boat on the river.
www.cooperslanding.net
573-657-2544

Visit Eagle Bluffs Conservation Area
Located south of Columbia, Eagle Bluffs offers a first-hand experience with man-made wetlands, which were created to help offset the loss of nearly 90 percent of Missouri's historical wetlands. Eight hundred acres of seasonal marshes and 450 acres of emergent marshes dot the area. Pierced Rock Natural Arch, described by Lewis and Clark in their journals, is visible along the Katy Trail here. The Missouri River once flowed through the area, and the steamship Plowboy *is believed to be buried under the sand and silt here.*
www.conservation.state.mo.us
573-884-6861

Visit Columbia, Missouri
Often called "College Town U.S.A.," because the University of Missouri, Stephens College, and Columbia College are located here, Columbia is a popular home base for exploring mid-Missouri's Lewis and Clark sites. In addition to more than twenty-six hotels, there are also several bed and breakfasts, gourmet restaurants, and an extensive variety of shops, museums, and galleries. A bronze sculpture of Thomas Jefferson is located on the quadrangle at the University of Missouri, as is Jefferson's original grave marker. The university was the

first public university founded in Jefferson's Louisiana Purchase territory. Also at the University is the Museum of Anthropology, which features American Indian artifacts from throughout Missouri.
www.visitcolumbiamo.com
573-875-1231

Near Rocheport, Missouri
June 6, 1804

The crew sets out this morning "under a Jentle Braise," after fixing the mast from their June 4 mishap. The men pass Saline Creek and note many salt licks. They also pass the mouth of Perche Creek, named for a natural feature known as *Roche Percee,* literally "hole in the rock" in French. Clark complains of a sore throat and a headache, and the Corps advances fourteen miles.

Visit Rocheport, Missouri
The small river town of Rocheport, French for "port of rocks," is often called the Gateway to the Katy Trail. The scenic, bluff-lined trail, panoramic views of the Missouri River, a blufftop winery, bike rentals, award-winning bed and breakfasts, and antiques shops make for an ideal weekend getaway. An old train tunnel that was blasted through solid rock is a particular highlight of this stretch of trail. The explorers saw pictographs in the bluffs as they passed by, but construction of the railroad tunnel likely led to their destruction. Rocheport holds an annual Lewis and Clark celebration on the weekend closest to June 7, the day Lewis and Clark passed through the area.
www.rocheport.com
573-698-3903

From top: A sculpture of Thomas Jefferson sits on the campus of the University of Missouri at Columbia. Graham Cave revealed signs of humans from more than ten thousand years ago.

Visit Diana Bend Conservation Area
Rocheport, Missouri
Diana Bend allows Katy Trail State Park visitors to view the Missouri River flood plain. When conditions are right, visitors can see herons, migratory shorebirds, and waterfowl.
573-884-6861

Near Boonville, Missouri
June 7, 1804

The crew passes the mouth of a creek they called the "Big Monitu," now known as Moniteau Creek, at present-day Rocheport. Above the mouth of this creek are "Several Courious Paintings and Carveing in the projecting rock of Limestone inlade with white red and blue flint." After making fourteen miles of progress, the crew camps at the mouth of Good Woman's River, now known as Bonne Femme Creek.

Visit New Franklin, Missouri
New Franklin is near the original site of Franklin, where the Santa Fe Trail originated. This small community also offers easy access to the Katy Roundhouse Restaurant and Campground.
www.katyroundhouse.com
800-477-6605

Visit Boonville, Missouri
Boonville is perhaps best known for its yearly Big Muddy Folk Festival at Thespian Hall. The Old Cobblestone Street under the Boonslick Bridge is considered the oldest paved street west of St. Louis, and Harley Park offers a view of the Big Muddy.
www.c-magic.com/boonvill/
660-882-2721

Visit Boone's Lick State Historic Site
Located twelve miles northwest of Boonville, Boone's Lick State Historic Site preserves a fifty-two acre site and the salty springs, or licks, where Nathan Boone and his brother Daniel Morgan Boone began manufacturing salt in 1805. The salt was a crucial meat preserver for pioneers heading west.
www.mostateparks.com/booneslick.htm
800-334-6946

Near Arrow Rock, Missouri
June 8, 1804

Today the men proceed twelve miles upriv-

Grand Pass Conservation Area, near Miami, Missouri, includes bottomland forests and wetlands, which are popular spots to view Canada geese and snow geese during winter.

er, passing two willow islands and a small creek. Nine miles into their day's progress, they pass the Mine River, known today as the Lamine River. Clark writes, "This river is about 70 yards wide at its mouth and is Said to be navagable for Perogues 80 or 90 ms ... The french inform that Lead Ore has been found in defferent parts of this river."

Visit Arrow Rock, Missouri
The site of Arrow Rock and its prominent bluffs were noted on French maps of the region as early as 1732 as "pierre fleche," or the "rock of arrows." Points of interest include the Arrow Rock State Historic Site museum, the restored home of artist George Caleb Bingham, and the Lyceum Theater.
www.arrowrock.org
660-837-3231

Near Lisbon, Missouri
June 9, 1804

After a heavy rain, Mother Nature tests the boat crew today. The men set out early into swift waters, and they are detained after hitting a snag. After passing the "Prarie of the Arrows," near present-day Arrow Rock, the crew faces a defining moment on the river. The boat's stern strikes a submerged log, and the current turns the boat against drifts and snags. Some of the men jump in the water

and swim to shore to steady the boat with a rope. Clark expresses pride at their confidence and quick teamwork.

Visit Glasgow, Missouri
Glasgow is remembered by early river men for being on the tightest bend in the Missouri River. But, as the story goes, the town was also beloved by boat crews, who enjoyed the fragrance of its flowers from a mile away. Sites of interest include the historic Lewis Library and the riverfront.
660-338-2377

Near Cambridge, Missouri
June 10-11, 1804

After a hard rain, the crew sets out very early this morning and passes several difficult stretches of river. Clark observes a number of goslings in the morning. The boats pass a bank, which begins to fall, taking many large cottonwood trees with it. The two captains walk about three miles into a "Country roleing open & rich, with plenty of water, great quantities of Deer. I discovered a Plumb which grows on bushes the hight of hasle," Clark writes. The Corps progresses ten miles today. Clark notes that he still has a "verry bad" cold. The hunters kill two deer and two bears, and Clark writes, "men verry lively Dancing & Singing."

On the Missouri River, south of Glasgow, June 9, 1804

"Set out early, water verry Swift got fast on a log, detained us ... Hard rain last night ... a pt. on the S. S. opposit the Commencement of the 1st Prarie, Called Prarie of the Arrows, the river at this place about 300 yds. ... The Current exceedingly Strong ... passed an Isld. In the mid R — in passing up on the S.S. opsd. The Isd. The Sturn of the boat Struck a log which was not proceiveable the Curt. Struck her bow and turn the boat against Some drift & Snags which below with great force; This was a disagreeable and Dangerous Situation, particularly as immense large trees were Drifting down and we lay imediately in their Course, — Some of our men being prepared for all Situations leaped into the water Swam ashore with a roap, and fixed themselves in Such Situations, that the boat was off in a fiew minits, I can Say with Confidence that our party is not inferior to any that was ever on the waters of the Missoppie. ... the Countrey on the S. S. high bottom & Delghtfull land." — William Clark

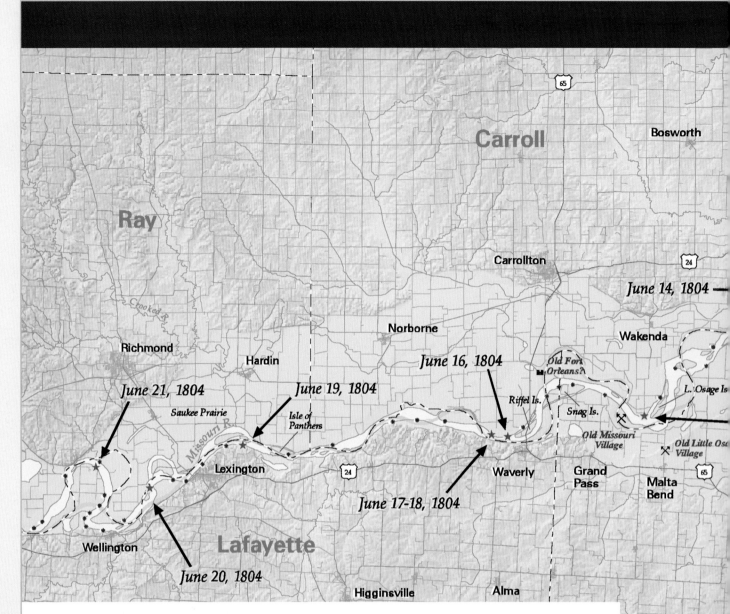

Carroll

Bosworth

Ray

Carrollton

June 14, 1804 —

Norborne

Wakenda

June 16, 1804

Old Fort
Orleans?

Richmond

Hardin

June 21, 1804

June 19, 1804

L. Osage Is

Riffel Is.

Saukee Prairie

Isle of
Panthers

Snag Is.

Missouri R.

Old Missouri
Village

Old Little Osc
Village

Lexington

Wellington

June 17-18, 1804

Waverly

Grand
Pass

Malta
Bend

Lafayette

June 20, 1804

Higginsville

Alma

June 12, 1804

After passing Plumb Creek, the crew halts to eat. Two small rafts come downriver from the Sioux nation. The Corps purchases three hundred pounds of "Voyagers Grece," most likely buffalo grease and tallow. They boats progress nine miles.

Near Brunswick, Missouri
June 13, 1804

Clark notes "a prarie in which the Missouries Indians once lived and the Spot where 300 of them fell a Sacrifise to the fury of the Saukees. This nation (Missouries) once the most noumerous nation in this part of the Continent now reduced to about eighty families." The men camp at the mouth of the Grand River.

Near Miami, Missouri
June 14, 1804

After setting out in a thick fog, the crew must again wrestle with the Mighty Mo. Clark writes, "The worst

place I have seen. A Sand bar makeing out 2/3 Cross the river Sand Collecting & forming Bars and Bars washg a way, the boat Struck and turned, She was near oversetting we saved her by Some extrodany exertions of our party (ever ready to inconture any fatigue for the premotion of the enterprise) ... Drewyer tels of a remarkable Snake inhabiting a Small lake 5 ms below which gobbles like a Turkey & may be herd Several miles. ..." Historians believe the snake story was likely a bit of folklore and not real.

Sweet
Springs

Visit Van Meter State Park and
State Historic Site
Miami, Missouri
Located twelve miles northwest of Marshall, the area of Van Meter State Park was the homeland of the Missouri Indians through the early 1700s. The 983-acre park includes a campground, hiking trails, and a fishing lake.
www.mostateparks.com/vanmeter.htm
800-334-6946

Pettis

0

Chariton

June 13, 1804

Brunswick

24

Keytesville

Salisb

erly

× Old Missouri
Village?

June 12, 1804

Miami

Chariton

June 10-11, 1804

1804

Slater

Chicot Is.

Glasgow

aline

Legend

★ Expedition Camp Sites

• Waypoints and Exploration Sites

⌂ Euro-American Towns and Villages

✕ Native American Settlements

⊞ Old Forts

◠ Historic Hydrography

〜 Present Big Rivers

Produced at the Geographic Resources Center,
Department of Geography, University of Missouri
Cartography by James D. Harlan
Copyright (C) Curators of the University of Missouri

SEAL OF THE SECRETARY OF STATE
MISSOURI

MU

MU Department of Geography
Geographic Resources Center

Fayette

Harrisburg

June 9, 1804

Marshall

Prairie of the Arrow

Arrow
Rock

Missouri R.

New Franklin

June 7, 1804

Boone

Rocheport

Arrow Rock
('Mills') Is.

65

Blackwater R.

Lamine R.

June 8, 1804

70

Boonville

Big Manitou Bluffs

June 6, 1804

Wooldridge

N
W   E
S

Big Manitou Is.

| 0 | 10 | 20 | 30 | 40 | 50 |

KILOMETERS

Lupus

| 10 | 20 | 30 | 40 | 50 |

MILES

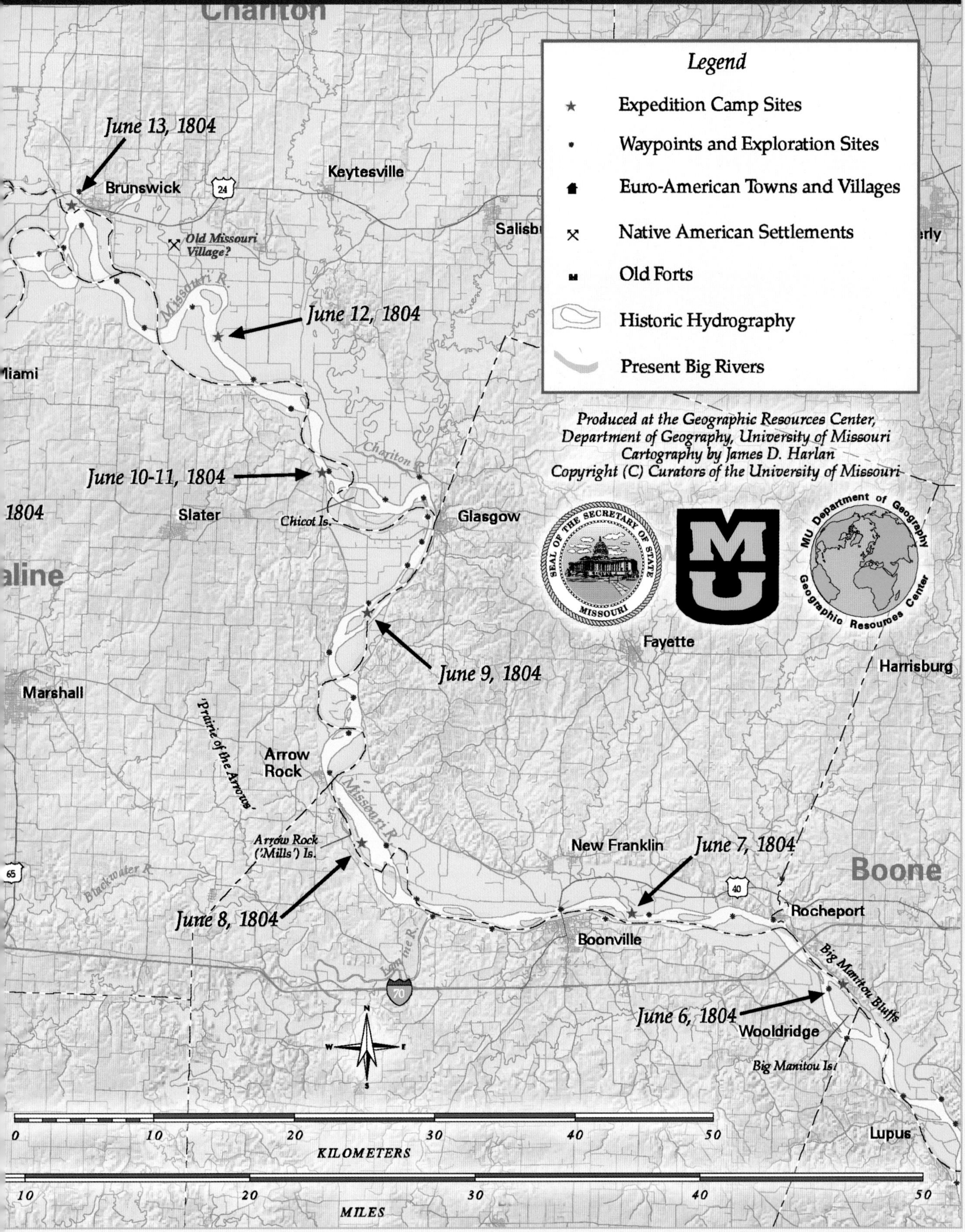

Visit Grand Pass Conservation Area
Near Miami, Missouri
At this fifty-three-hundred-acre site, a braided series of levees, roads, and trails offers the chance to view waterfowl, migratory birds, shorebirds, geese, and ducks.
660-595-2444

Near Grand Pass, Missouri
June 15, 1804

The crew sets out early, and before long the boat wheels around on a sawyer (a sunken log), "which was near injuring us Verry much … near doeing her great damage … the river is riseing fast & the water exceedingly Swift," Clark writes. "This is said to be the worst part of the river." The expedition proceeds twelve and one-fourth miles today.

Near Waverly, Missouri
June 16, 1804

The crew progresses ten miles despite a sand bar that Clark describes as "the worst I had Seen which the boat must pass or Drop back Several Miles & Stem a Swift Current on the opsd Side of an isd [island]." Once the boat got there, however, it "assended the middle of the Streem which was diffucult Dangerious We Came to above this place at

Dark and Camped in a bad place, the misquitoes and Ticks are noumerous and bad."

June 17-18, 1804

The better part of the day is spent making oars and a new towrope. Clark measures the current of the river at this place by floating a stick downriver and timing it. He notes that much of the party is afflicted with boils and several have dysentery.

Near Lexington, Missouri
June 19, 1804

After a rainy night, the crew finishes the new oars, sets out under a gentle breeze and passes two large islands. Clark observes gooseberries and raspberries along the shore in great abundance. The crew makes seventeen and a half miles progress.

Visit Lexington, Missouri
Lexington, founded in 1822, was the original headquarters of Russell, Majors & Waddell, the primary outfitters for the Santa Fe Trail. Today Lexington is best known for Wentworth Military Academy, more than 130 antebellum homes, and the Lafayette County Courthouse.
www.historiclexington.com
660-259-4711

Visit the Battle of Lexington State Historic Site and the Anderson House
Lexington, Missouri
This 106-acre Civil War battle site preserves the remnants of the trenches and the graves of unknown Union troops. The Anderson House, which played a major role in the battle, was built here in 1853 and is also open for tours.
www.mostateparks.com/lexington/lexington.htm
800-334-6946

June 20, 1804

The men enjoy a gentle breeze as they navigate swift water, and they travel about seven miles. Clark writes: "The Swet run off our men in a Strem when they row hard." Clark also notes a large, beautiful prairie called Sauke Prairie and a sandbar ahead "over which the water riffleed and roered like a great fall." In another entry from the same day, Clark writes of seeing pelicans on a sandbar and writes, "my servant York nearly loseing an eye by a man throwing sand into it. … Land appeard verry good on each Side of the River to day and well timbered. … a butifull night but the air exceedingly Damp & the mosquiters verry troublesom."

Visit Wellington, Missouri

Once best-known for coal mining, the town was probably named for the Duke of Wellington, who defeated Napoleon at Waterloo. The small town includes historic homes, antiques, and a city park at the center of town that features a monument to the Santa Fe Trail.

Near Camden, Missouri
June 21, 1804

The river rises three inches overnight, and the water is swift and dangerous. As they maneuver around a small island, the men must row, push with poles, and draw the boat with a strong rope. Clark writes, "we assended without wheeling or receving any damige more than breakeing one of my starboard Windows. …" Clark also confirms whether the Big Muddy has always been, as Mark Twain later put it, "too thick to drink, too thin to plow." Clark writes, "The Common water of the missourie … contains half a Comn Wine Glass of ooze or mud to every pint." At the day's end, the crew is rewarded with a classic Missouri sunset. "The atmespier presented every appearance of wind, Blue & white Streeks Centering at the Sun as She disappeared and the Clouds Situated to the S.W., Guilded in the most butifull manner."

Visit Napoleon, Missouri

Originally called Poston's Landing, this small river town was platted in 1836 as Napoleon. Its name changed to Lisbon in 1857, but like many other towns, the post office name had already been chosen, and so the town's official name remained Napoleon. Visitors should stop at the G&S General Store, a 110-year-old business that offers groceries, farm supplies, and an old-fashioned deli. Shoppers should also visit Ma and Pa's Riverview Antiques Mall, in a historic building right across the street from the general store.

Near Levasy, Missouri
June 22, 1804

The river rises four inches overnight. Clark writes, "I was waken'd before day light this morning by the guard prepareing the boat to receve an apparent Storm which threttened violence from the West. at day light a violent wind accompanied with rain came from the W. and lasted about one hour. …" When the storm clears, the men set out and pass swift water crowded with snags, two large islands, and a "large &extensive Prarie on the Labd. Side" that Clark says is "butifull." Lewis walks on shore for a few miles this afternoon. In mid-afternoon, a thermometer reads eighty-seven degrees. After ten and a half miles, the boat crews reach the mouth of a large creek called the River of the Fire Prairie, where they reunite with Pvts. John Shields and John Collins, who had set out hunting the day before. Shields and Collins inform the captains that the lands they passed through while hunting were "fine and well watered."

Near Sibley, Missouri
June 23, 1804

After the men stop at an island, a hard wind blowing downriver prevents them from

A cannonball that struck the Lexington Courthouse during the three-day 1861 Civil War battle at the site is still visible. The battlefield has been preserved as a state historic site. The site includes remnants of trenches used in the battle and graves of unknown Union soldiers.

On the Missouri River, near Parkville, June 29, 1804

"a Court martial will Set this day at 11 oClock, to Consist of five members, for the trial of John Collins and Hugh Hall, Confined on Charges exhibited against them by Sergeant Floyd, agreeable to the articles of War. The Court Convened agreeable to order and proceeded to the trial of the Prisoners Viz John Collins Charged 'with getting drunk on his post this morning out of whiskey put under his Charge as a Sentinal and for Suffering Hugh Hall to draw whiskey out of the Said Barrel intended for the party' To this Charge the prisoner plead not guilty. The Court after mature deliveration on the evidence abduced ... are of oppinion that the prisoner is Guilty of the Charge exhibited against him, and do therefore Sentence him to recive one hundred Lashes on his bear Back. Hugh Hall was brought with 'taking whiskey out of a Keg this morning which whiskey was Stored on the Bank (and under the Charge of the guard) Contrary to all order, rule, or regulation' To this Charge the prisoner 'Pleades Guilty.' The Court find the prisoner guilty and Sentence him to receive fifty lashes on his bear Back. The Commanding Officers approve of the Sentence of the Court and orders that the Punishment take place at half past three this evening, at which time the party will Parrade for inspection." — William Clark

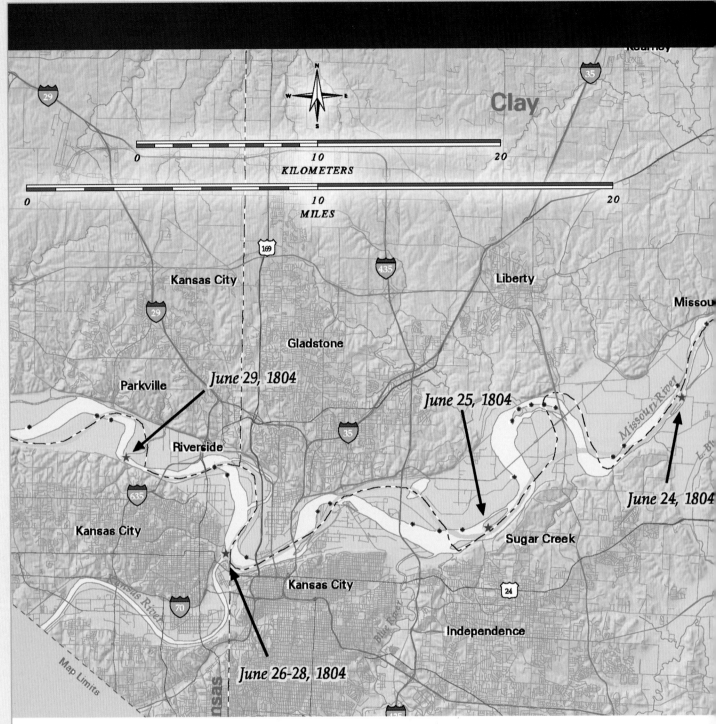

Clay

KILOMETERS

MILES

Kansas City

Liberty

Missou

Gladstone

June 29, 1804

Parkville

June 25, 1804

Riverside

June 24, 1804

Kansas City

Sugar Creek

Kansas City

Independence

June 26-28, 1804

leaving it. Clark gets out of the boat to walk on shore, planning to meet the party later in the day. He walks around an extensive bend in the river, kills a deer, and makes a fire. He expects the boats to come upriver in the evening, but "the wind continueing to blow prevented their moveing, as the distance by land was too great for me to return by night, I concluded to Camp, Peeled Some bark to lay on, and geathered wood to make fires to Keep off the musquitor & Knats. Heard the party on Shore fire, at Dark, Drewyer came to

me with the horses, one fat bear & a Deer, river fell 8 Inches last night." The boats move forward only three miles.

Visit Sibley, Missouri
This town was platted by Archibald Gamble in 1836 and named for his brother-in-law, George Sibley, who commanded Fort Sibley at the site from 1818 to 1826. The town once boasted the only Missouri River ferry west of Lexington, but it was severely damaged by floods in 1844 and again by Union forces in 1863. Today this small community

acts as a gateway to Fort Osage.

Visit Fort Osage
Sibley, Missouri
After noting the promising location for a fort on the return trip of his expedition with Lewis, Clark returned to this site in 1808 with Captain Eli Clemson to erect a fort. It served several purposes: it included a trade house to sell and trade with American Indians, it functioned as an outpost in the newly acquired Louisiana Purchase, it housed soldiers to guard the new territory,

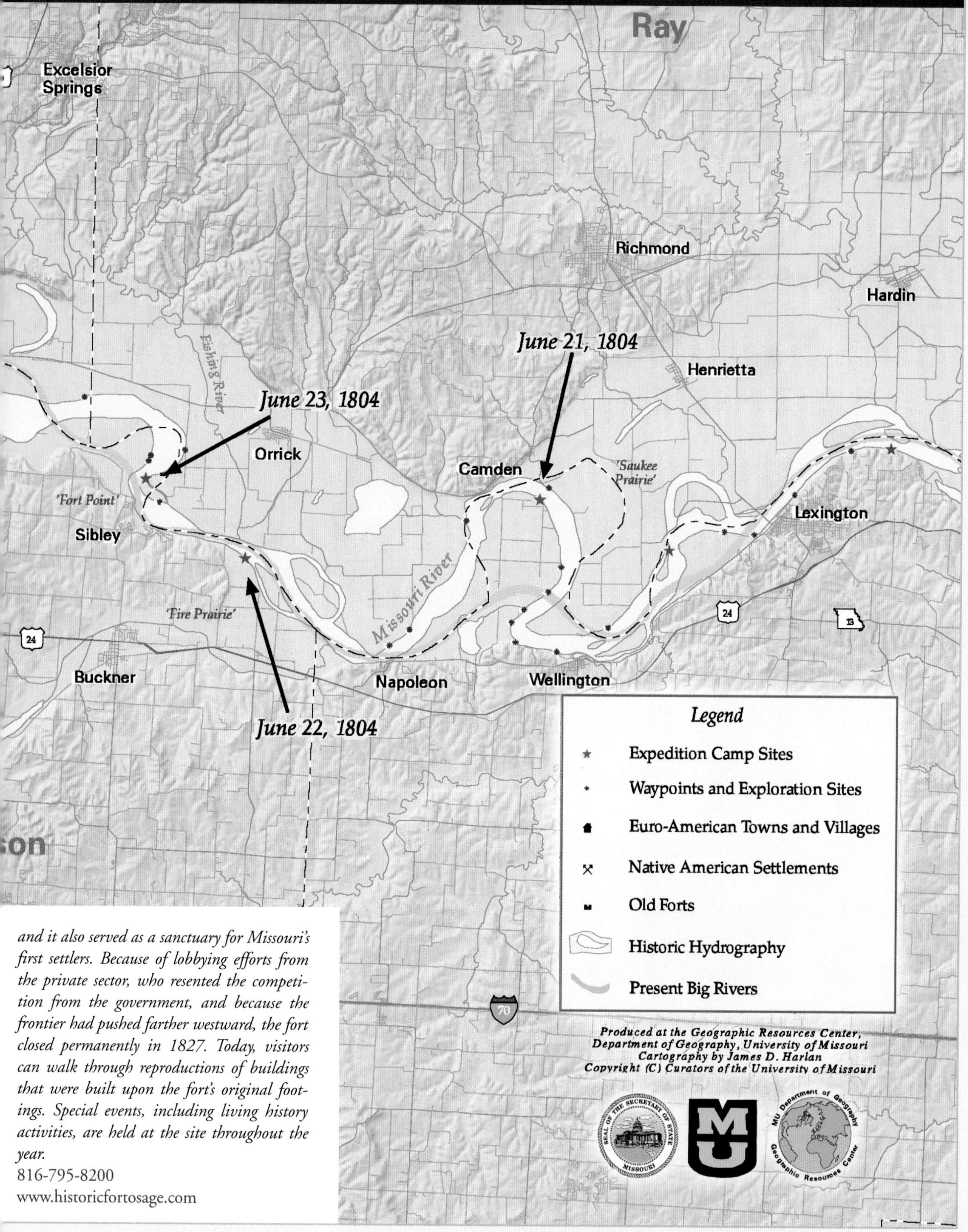

Ray

Excelsior
Springs

Richmond

Hardin

Fishing River

June 21, 1804

June 23, 1804

Henrietta

Orrick

Camden

'Saukee
Prairie'

'Fort Point'

Lexington

Sibley

Missouri River

'Fire Prairie'

24

13

June 22, 1804

Buckner

Napoleon

Wellington

24

70

Legend

★ Expedition Camp Sites

✦ Waypoints and Exploration Sites

🏠 Euro-American Towns and Villages

✗ Native American Settlements

🏰 Old Forts

〰 Historic Hydrography

〰 Present Big Rivers

Produced at the Geographic Resources Center,
Department of Geography, University of Missouri
Cartography by James D. Harlan
Copyright (C) Curators of the University of Missouri

and it also served as a sanctuary for Missouri's first settlers. Because of lobbying efforts from the private sector, who resented the competition from the government, and because the frontier had pushed farther westward, the fort closed permanently in 1827. Today, visitors can walk through reproductions of buildings that were built upon the fort's original footings. Special events, including living history activities, are held at the site throughout the year.

816-795-8200

www.historicfortosage.com

From top: The world headquarters of the Community of Christ is at Independence. Clark established Fort Osage in 1808. A statue overlooks the confluence of the Kansas and Missouri Rivers at Kansas City, where Lewis and Clark camped in June 1804.

Visit Cooley Lake Conservation Area
Near Liberty, Missouri
This 917-acre site is one of the few remaining oxbow lakes on the western part of the Missouri River in the state. Shorebirds, waterfowl, and wading birds migrating along the Missouri River gather here. The area attracts egrets, bitterns, black-crowned night herons, green herons, great blue herons, and mallard and wood ducks. The best times to view the migrations are during the spring and early fall.
816-530-5500
www.conservation.state.mo.us

Near Atherton, Missouri
June 24, 1804

Clark writes about his brief adventure away from the boats on June 23 in more detail: "I concld to hunt on a Willow Isl. Situated close under the Shore, in Crossing from an Island, I got mired, and was obliged to Craul out, a disagreeable Situation & a Diverting one of any one who Could have Seen me after I got out, all Covered with mud." The men on the river pass between two sandbars at the head of which the crew must get out and raise the boat eight inches to pass. After about eleven miles of progress, the men camp on an island. Clark notes that the party is in high spirits.

Visit Independence, Missouri
Founded in 1827, Independence is home to attractions such as the Harry S. Truman National Historic Site, which includes the Truman Home, known during Truman's presidency as the "Summer White House." At the National Frontier Trails Center, visitors can learn about the three great routes that led pioneers west. Independence is known as the "Queen City of Trails," because it served as a launching point for travelers on the Santa Fe, Oregon, and California Trails.
800-748-7323
www.ci.independence.mo.us

Near Kansas City, Missouri
June 25, 1804

The river falls another eight inches overnight, and fog detains the crew for about an hour. Clark notes a bank on the larboard side, which "appears to Contain a great quantity of excellente Coal." The crew passes a small creek called Bennet's Creek.

Clark writes, "The Prairies Come within a Short distance of the river on each Side which Contains in addition to Plumbs Raspberries & vast quantities of wild crab apples and wild flowers. Great numbers of Deer are seen feeding on the young willows & earbage in the Banks and on the Sand bars in the river." The hunters and shore party do not rejoin the boat crew this evening. The crew progresses thirteen miles.

Visit Kansas City, Missouri
High above the confluence of the Missouri and Kansas Rivers, Case Park offers a unique vantage point from which to view the city and includes a bronze sculpture of Lewis, Clark, York, Sacagawea, and Lewis's dog, Seaman. The nearby Kansas City Riverfront Park offers views of the Missouri River and the eighteen-mile Riverfront Heritage Trail for pedestrians and bikers. Other area highlights for Lewis and Clark aficionados include Westport's Pioneer Park and the Country Club Plaza's Discovery Center, which features a Lewis and Clark mural, movie, and a model of the keelboat.
www.visitkc.com
www.journey4th.org
800-767-7700

June 26-28, 1804

Clark notes that this stretch of the river is confined to a very narrow channel. The men kill a large rattlesnake that they see sunning itself on the riverbank, and their towrope breaks twice as they try to pull the boat through rough waters. The crew camps at a point above the confluence of the Kansas and Missouri Rivers. Clark observes a great number of "Parrot queets," or Carolina parakeets, which are now extinct. The explorers decide to stay at this spot for a few days to rest, take measurements of the Kansas River, and dry and repair the boats.

June 29, 1804

The boats run into rough water, and when the keelboat strikes a shifting sandbar, it comes close to hitting a snag that Clark says could have caused the boat to sink. Two men are court-martialed for stealing and drinking whiskey from the crew's supplies. They are found guilty, and each is sentenced to "Lashes on his bear back."

From left: Weston Bend State Park offers one of the most expansive views of the Missouri River in the state. The Pony Express statue in St. Joseph honors the historic mail route that began there in 1860 and extended all the way to Sacramento, California.

Near Kansas City, Missouri
June 30, 1804

The crew passes the mouth of the "Petite Plate" (today's Platte or Little Platte River). After traveling about ten miles, the men camp opposite the lower point of Diamond Island. Clark finishes the day's log with three words: "Broke our mast."

Visit Parkville, Missouri

Parkville's English Landing Park is full of walking trails with river views. Just steps away, the riverfront business district offers shopping, dining, and a farmer's market.
www.parkvillemo.com
816-741-7676

Near Farley, Missouri
July 1, 1804

A soldier on night patrol sounds an alarm after being "challenged" by either a man or a beast, who then runs off mysteriously. The crew stops for a three-hour break in the excessive July heat. Clark notes seeing "PueCanns," or pecan trees and also "great quantities of raspburies an Grapes."

Near Weston, Missouri
July 2, 1804

The crew passes on the left of the "Isles des parques." Clark supposes the sudden crowding of drift is due to the caving in of the banks of an island upriver. They pass Turkey Creek and "a large Island ... Called by the Inds. Wau-car-ba war-con-da or the Bear Medison Island." They spend four hours in the heat making a new mast from a cottonwood tree, and they camp opposite the "1st old Village of the Kanzes ..."

Visit Weston Bend State Park
Near Weston, Missouri

Take your time exploring this 1,133-acre park and its scenic Missouri River overlook. The park offers excellent bird-watching during spring and fall migrations.
www.mostateparks.com/westonbend.htm
800-334-6946

Visit Weston, Missouri

The tobacco crop and the river port brought early success to Weston, which by 1858 was recognized as the world's largest hemp port. Today, the antebellum homes, winery, museums, and the only tobacco auction west of the Mississippi River draw many visitors. Lewis and Clark Trad'n Days are held the last weekend of June each year.
ci.weston.mo.us
888-635-7457

Near Lewis and Clark, Missouri
July 3, 1804

The men pass a large island called *Isle Vache* or "Cow Island." They stop at a deserted trading house on the river, and there they find "a verry fat hourse, which appears to have been lost a long time."

Near Rushville, Missouri
July 4, 1804

The crew "ussered in the day by a discharge of one shot from our Bow piece," to celebrate the Fourth of July. This is considered the first official observance of the holiday in the newly acquired Louisiana Purchase territory. Clark writes of naming a nearby creek "Independence us. Creek." The men

North of St. Joseph, Missouri, July 7, 1804

"Set out early passed Some verry Swift water on the L.S. which Compelled us to Draw up by the Cord. a verry warm morning, passed a butifull Prarie on the right Side which extends back, those Praries has much the appearance from the river of farms, Divided by narrow Strips of woods those Strips of timber grows along the runs which rise on the hill & pass to the river a Cleft above, one man sick (Frasure) Struck with the Sun, Saw a large rat on the Side of the bank, Killed a wolf on the Bank passed a verry narrow part of the river, all confined within 200 yards, a yellow bank above, passed a Small willow Island. ... a pond on the S. S near the prarie we passed yesterday in which G D. Saw Several young Swans we Came to and Camped on the L.S. and two men Sent out last evening with the horses did not Join us this evening agreeable to orders — a hard wind with Some rain from the N, E at 7 oClock which lasted half an hour, with thunder & lightning. river fall a little" —William Clark

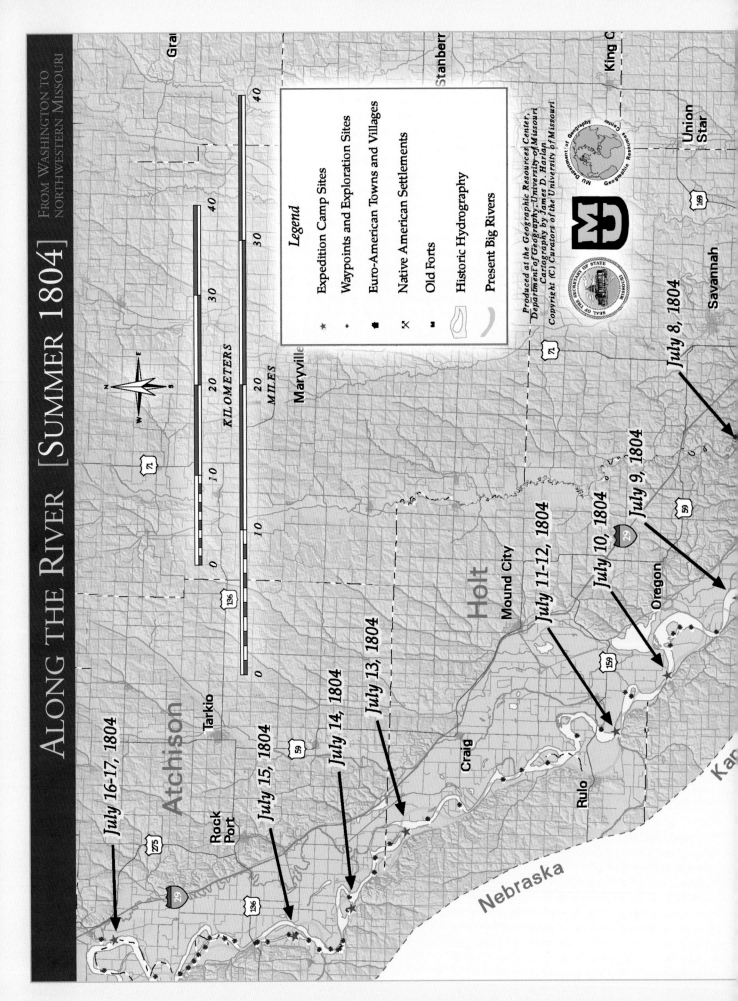

ALONG THE RIVER [SUMMER 1804]

Legend

★ Expedition Camp Sites

✦ Waypoints and Exploration Sites

◆ Euro-American Towns and Villages

✕ Native American Settlements

■ Old Forts

Historic Hydrography

Present Big Rivers

Produced at the Geographic Resources Center,
Department of Geography, University of Missouri
Cartography by James D. Harlan
Copyright (C) Curators of the University of Missouri

KILOMETERS

MILES

July 16-17, 1804

July 15, 1804

July 14, 1804

July 13, 1804

July 11-12, 1804

July 10, 1804

July 9, 1804

July 8, 1804

Atchison

Holt

Tarkio

Rock Port

Craig

Rulo

Mound City

Oregon

Maryville

Savannah

Union Star

Nebraska

Kan

Stewartsville

Plattst

Cl

June 29, 1804

Gladstone

Gower

169

Smithville

135

St. Joseph

July 6, 1804

July 5, 1804

Buchanan

29

Platte

June 30, 1804

Kansas City

36

July 4, 1804

July 3, 1804

July 2, 1804

Platte City

July 1, 1804

435

59

Weston

73

36

Troy

Old Kanzas Village

Old Kanzas Village & Old Fort Cavagnial

Leavenworth

Kansas

73

Atchison

---

end the day with another discharge from the bow piece and "an extra Gill of whiskey."

Visit Lewis and Clark State Park
Near Rushville, Missouri

The lake that Clark described on July 4, 1804, is known today as Lewis and Clark Lake. Lewis and Clark State Park borders this lake. Waterfowl still flock to the lake, including geese, great blue herons, snowy egrets, and ducks. A swimming beach, picnic spots, playground, and camping areas are also available.
www.mostateparks.com/lewisandclark.htm
800-334-6946

July 5, 1804
The crew passes the former site of a Kansas Indian town. Clark writes, "The Cause of those people moveing from this place I cannot learn, but naterally conclude that War has reduced their nation & compelled them to retire further into the Plains."

July 6, 1804
On this very warm day, Clark writes, "I observe that the men Swet more than is Common from Some Cause, I think the Missouries water is the principal Cause."

Near St. Joseph, Missouri
July 7, 1804
The boats pass through swift waters and then a prairie called "St. Michul." A hunter kills a wolf, and the crew camps for the night after progressing fourteen miles.

Visit St. Joseph, Missouri

"St. Joe," is where the Pony Express began, and where Jesse James met his demise. Today's travelers should visit the town's many museums, historic homes, and scenic riverfront.
www.stjomo.com
800-785-0360

Near Green Valley, Missouri
July 8, 1804
Clark writes, "five men sick today with a violent Head ake. and Several with Boils." The men stop to eat and camp at

From left: Interpretive signs like this one at Weston mark the spots where Lewis and Clark camped throughout the state. More than three hundred species of birds stop to rest and rejuvenate at Squaw Creek National Wildlife Refuge during annual spring and fall migrations.

an island called Nadawa, which Clark calls "the largest I have Seen in the river."

July 9, 1804
The boats pass Wolf River. The men set up camp opposite an island, and the flicker of a campfire alerts them to another party on the opposite shore. The men try to signal the unknown party, and when the other camp does not answer, the captains suspect that it might be a Sioux war party.

Near Forest City, Missouri
July 10, 1804
The other camp was actually comprised of the expedition's hunters, who had turned in early and had not heard the crew's signal attempts due to the strong wind. Clark calls it "a mistake altogether." The crew stops on Solomon's Island to eat. "Our men all getting well but much fatigued," Clark writes.

Visit Squaw Creek
National Wildlife Refuge
Mound City, Missouri
This seven-thousand-acre refuge, established in 1935, is a popular wintering area for bald eagles and snow geese, and it provides habitat for more than three hundred species of birds.
midwest.fws.gov/SquawCreek
660-442-3187

July 11, 1804
The crew sets out early, passing a willow island and Little Tarkio Creek. The men kill seven deer and camp on an island opposite the Nemaha River after traveling six miles.

July 12, 1804
The captains let the men rest today while they take observations of their surroundings. Clark takes five men to explore up the Nemaha for about three miles. On a sandstone cliff, Clark marks his name and day of the month. Alexander Willard is tried for sleeping on his post. As his punishment, he receives twenty-five lashes at sunset for the next four days.

July 13, 1804
After being rocked by a violent storm during the night, the crew sets out at sunrise. Clark notes a beautiful and extensive prairie covered with grass and abounding with grapes of "defferent kinds." They travel more than twenty miles today.

July 14, 1804
Hard showers delay the crew's departure. Shortly after they set out, "a Violent Storm … Struck the boat … aded to a Strong Cable and Anchor was Scrcely Sufficient to Keep the boat from being thrown up on the

Sand Island." They continued for forty minutes and "this Storm Suddenly Seased, & 1 minit the river was as Smoth as glass."

Near Langdon, Missouri
July 15, 1804
Clark travels overland across streams, high prairies, lands "covered with pea Vine & rich weed" and past the Little Nemaha. He swims across it, hikes another three miles, and then waits for the boats. The men progress almost ten miles.

July 16, 1804
After setting out early, the crew passes several small islands, and the boat runs atop a sawyer. Clark describes a spot "where about 20 acres of the hill has latterly Sliped into the river above a clift of Sand Stone. … the resort of burds of Different Kinds to reare their young." He also notes a large "Ball pated Prarie." The men travel twenty miles.

July 17, 1804
The crew rests today so that the captains can ascertain their longitude. Several men are sent out to hunt. Lewis returns from a hike, noting "hand Som Countrey." The men camp in the "Bald Pated Prarie," and the next day, they leave the land that will later become the state of Missouri.

[FALL 1806]

THE RETURN TRIP THROUGH MISSOURI

September 9, 1806

Having sent the keelboat back downriver in 1805, the expedition returns to Missouri in a flotilla of canoes. They pass what is now the Iowa-Missouri state line and the Platte River, and the river becomes more rapid and turbulent as they descend. In the evening, the crew camps at the "Bald pated prairie," which Clark noted on July 16, 1804, on the trip up the Missouri River. Clark mentions that Captain Lewis has recovered from being accidentally shot in the thigh in August. He also notes that the mosquitoes are less of a nuisance than they had been upriver and that the weather is becoming warmer every day. The men are eager to return home, and the crew travels seventy-three miles today before making camp.

Near Big Lake, Missouri
September 10, 1806

The crew sets out under a moderate wind and meets three Frenchmen heading upriver in a pirogue to trade with the "Pania Luup, or Wolf Indians." Clark listens to news of Zebulon Pike's explorations on the Mississippi River and his expedition up the Arkansas River. Clark writes, "we find the river in this timbered Country narrow and more moveing Sands and a much greater quantity of Sawyers or Snags than above. … we Saw Deer rackoons and turkies on the Shores to day one of the men killed a racoon which the indians very much admired." The men travel sixty-five miles.

Near Amazonia, Missouri
September 11, 1806

The Corps travels forty miles today. The remaining meat supply has spoiled, so the crew stops before reaching the Nodaway River to send out six hunters. The hunters are only able to bring in two deer, despite seeing abundant deer sign. Clark notes, "the mosquitoes are no longer troublesome on the river, from what cause they are noumerous above and not So on this part

of the river I cannot account." He writes about the "wolves howling in different directions … the barking of the little prarie wolves resembled those of our Common Small Dogs. … The papaws nearly ripe."

Near St. Joseph, Missouri
September 12, 1806

After traveling seven miles, the crew encounters more trappers paddling up the river. At St. Michael's Prairie (present-day St. Joseph) Clark meets with two French interpreters, Pierre Dorion, a Sioux interpreter, and Joseph Gravelines, who had previously assisted the expedition. In the spring of 1805, Gravelines had escorted an Arikara chief to Washington, D.C. Clark learns the unfortunate news that the chief died on the journey. He tells Gravelines to invite a dozen other upriver chiefs to visit Washington, D.C., the following spring. He writes, "the evening proveing to be wet and Cloudy we Concluded to continue all night, we despatched the two Canoes a head to hunt with 5 hunters in them."

September 13, 1806

The men set out shortly after sunrise. Soon, they reunite with the five hunters, who had not caught any game. A hard wind prevents the men from proceeding safely through the snags in the river. A few hours later, the hunters bring in four deer and a turkey, despite complaints of rushes so high and thick that it was impossible to kill a deer. They proceed eighteen miles on this "disagreeably worm" day.

September 14, 1806

The crew sets out early and all men are prepared for an encounter with the Kansa, or Kaw, Indians, who often exact a bribe for passage or rob boats outright on this part of the river. Below the old Kansa village, they meet three large boats bound for trade with the Yanktons and Mahars. Clark writes, "those young men received us with great friendship and pressed on us Some whisky

From top: Lewis and Clark's restaurant is in historic downtown St. Charles. Fort Osage, which Clark established after the journey, is visible from the Missouri River.

for our men, Bisquet, Pork and Onions & part of their Stores, we continued near 2 hours with those boats, makeing every enquirey into the state of our friends and Country." After descending a total of fifty-three miles, they stop at an island, where they "Sung Songs untill 11 oClock at night in the greatest harmoney."

Near Missouri City, Missouri
September 15, 1806

After setting out early under a stiff head wind, the men see several deer swimming in the river and pass the mouth of the Kansas River. Clark writes, "about a mile

The return trip down the Missouri River, September 9, 1806

"The river bottoms are extencive rich and Covered with tall large timber, and the hollows of the reveins may be Said to be covered with timber Such as Oake ash Elm and Some walnut & hickory. our party appears extreamly anxious to get on, and every day appears produce new anxieties in them to get to their Country and friends. My worth friend Cap Lewis has entirely recovered his wounds are heeled up and he Can walk and even run nearly as well as ever he Could. ... The Musquetors are yet troublesom, tho' not So much So as they were above the River platt. the Climate is every day preceptably wormer and air more Sultery than I have experienced for a long time. the nights are now So worm that I sleep Comfortable under a thin blanket, a fiew days past 2 was not more than Sufficient." —William Clark

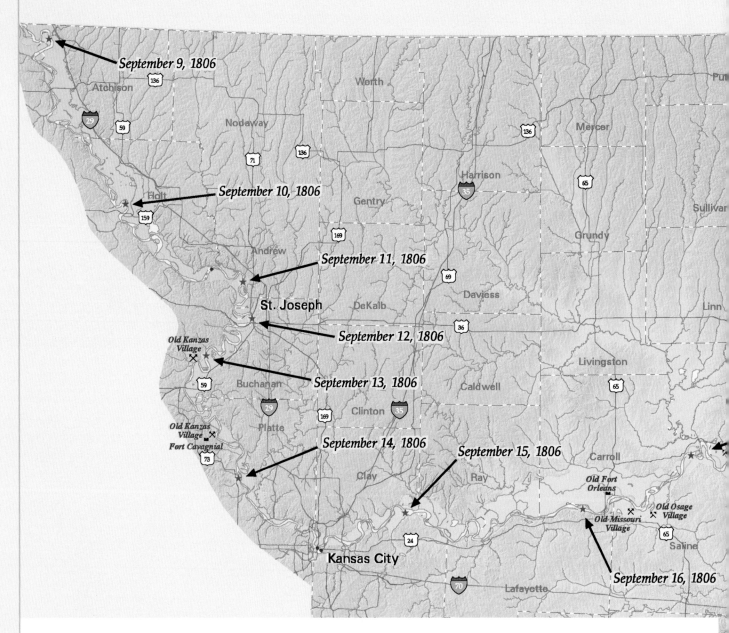

September 9, 1806

Atchison

September 10, 1806

Holt

September 11, 1806

St. Joseph

September 12, 1806

Old Kanzas Village

September 13, 1806

Buchanan

September 14, 1806

September 15, 1806

Carroll

Old Fort Orleans

Old Osage Village

Old Missouri Village

Saline

September 16, 1806

Kansas City

Lafayette

below we landed and Capt Lewis and my Self assended a hill which appeared to have a Commanding Situation for a fort, the Shore is bold and rocky imediately at the foot of the hill, from the top of the hill you have a perfect Command of the river. ..." Several hunters team up to hunt and kill a small elk. Due to strong winds, they descend only forty-nine miles. Clark notes, "we passd Some of the most Charming bottom lands to day. ... the weather disagreeably worm ... we Should be almost

Suficated Comeing out of a northern Country open and Cool ... in which we had been for nearly two years, rapidly decending into a woody Country in a wormer Climate ... is probably the Cause of our experiencing the heat much more ... than those who have Continued within [it]. ..."

September 16, 1806

The day proves to be "excessively worm and disagreeable." The men meet young Joseph Robidoux, bound for trade with the Panias,

Mahars, and Otos. Robidoux, whose family had been leaders in the fur trade for several generations, had established a trading post at the site of St. Joseph in 1800. The expedition party camps at an island after traveling fifty-two miles downriver today.

Near Miami, Missouri
September 17, 1806

The explorers pass the island of the Little Osage village. Clark writes, "at this place water of the Missouri is confined between

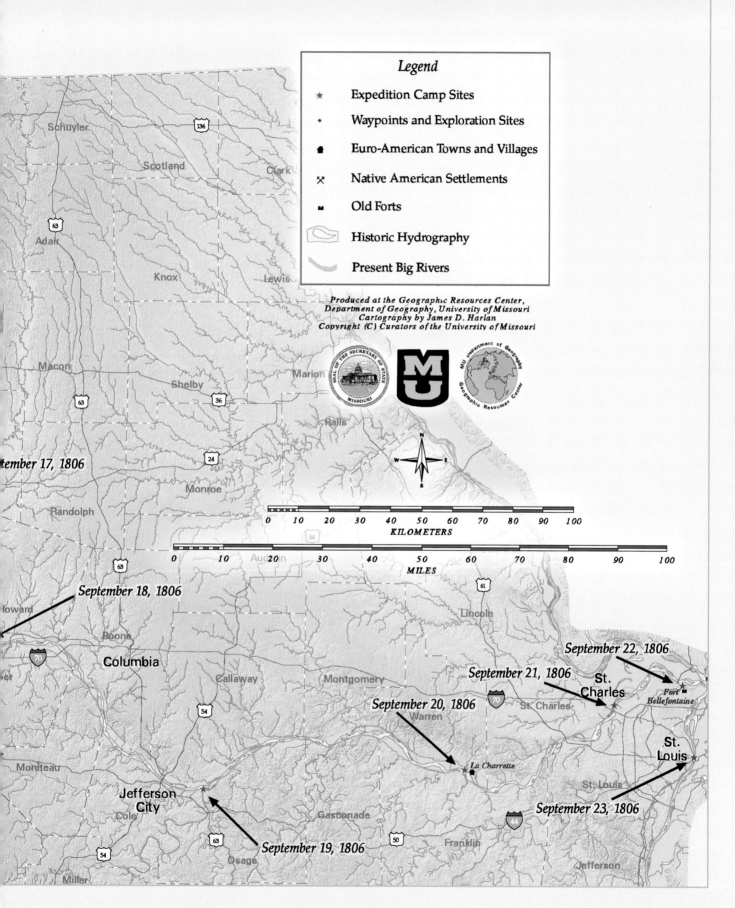

Legend

★ Expedition Camp Sites

⁕ Waypoints and Exploration Sites

⬟ Euro-American Towns and Villages

✕ Native American Settlements

⌂ Old Forts

Historic Hydrography

Present Big Rivers

*Produced at the Geographic Resources Center,
Department of Geography, University of Missouri
Cartography by James D. Harlan
Copyright (C) Curators of the University of Missouri*

KILOMETERS

0 10 20 30 40 50 60 70 80 90 100

MILES

0 10 20 30 40 50 60 70 80 90 100

September 17, 1806

September 18, 1806

September 19, 1806

September 20, 1806

September 21, 1806

September 22, 1806

September 23, 1806

an Island and the SE main Shore and passes through a narrow chanel for more than 2 miles which is crouded with Snags in maney places. ..." The party meets Capt. John McClellan and his crew, who are heading upriver. McClellan "was Somewhat astonished to See us return and appeared rejoiced to meet us. ... this Gentleman informed us that we had been long Since given out by the people of the U S Generaly and almost forgotten, the President of the U. States had yet hopes of us. ..." The men travel thirty miles and camp four miles above the Grand River.

September 18, 1806

The crew rises early and passes the Grand River. They stop to gather potatoes, as they are low on food. Clark writes, "We have nothing but a fiew Buisquit to eate and are partly compelled to eate poppows. ..." They see little game today: one deer, a bear at a distance, and three turkeys. Several crew members complain of sore eyes. The men travel fifty-two miles.

Near Jefferson City, Missouri
September 19, 1806

Clark writes, "we decended with great velocity. ... our anxiety as also the wish of the party to proceed on as expeditiously as possible ... enduce us to continue on without halting to hunt." Clark calculates that the first settlement they will encounter is still 140 miles downriver. They hope to reach it in two days. They cover seventy-two miles and camp at the confluence of the Osage River. The crew's eye irritation persists, likely caused by the papaws, although Clark suspects it could be from "the reflection of the Sun on the water."

Near Marthasville, Missouri
September 20, 1806

This morning, three crewman are unable to row due to the sorry state of their eyes. "We found it necessary to leave one of our Crafts and divide the men into the other Canoes," Clark writes. They pass the mouth of the Osage River and then the Gasconade River. They also pass five Frenchmen on a pirogue heading upriver. Later in the day, they come upon the small French village of La Charrette. "The men raised a Shout and

Sprung upon their ores and we soon landed opposit to the Village. our party requested to be permited to fire off their Guns which was alowed & they discharged 3 rounds with a harty Cheer. ..." Lewis and Clark quickly procure pork, beef, and whiskey for the crew. The people in the village are thrilled to see the explorers, who had been presumed lost. The men travel sixty-eight miles downriver today.

St. Charles, Missouri
September 21, 1806

After setting out, the men pass twelve canoes of Kickapoos ascending the river on

From top: The men passed the lush land that is now part of Missouri's wine country. The state capital is named for Thomas Jefferson, who commissioned the journey.

a hunting expedition. Clark writes, "Saw Several persons also Stock of different kind on the bank which reviv'd the party very much. At 4 p.m. we arived in Sight of St. Charles, the party rejoiced at the Sight of this hospital village plyed thear ores with great dexterity. ... we Saluted the Village by three rounds from our blunderbuts and the Small arms of the party. ... the inhabitants of this village appear much delighted at our return and seem to vie with each other in their politeness to us all." The men travel forty-eight miles today.

September 22, 1806

Because of heavy rain, the party decides not to set out as early as usual. Clark takes this opportunity to write to his friends in Kentucky. When the rain ceases, the men set out for Fort Bellefontaine at St. Louis.

St. Louis, Missouri
September 23, 1806

The crew descends to the Mississippi River and down to St. Louis, where they "received a harty welcom. ..." The explorers then visit Peter Chouteau and other friends, grateful to have returned safely after traveling nearly eight thousand miles — and for more than a thousand days since they first set foot in Missouri — on an adventure that would become an American legend.